Unconventional
Warrior

P9-CJK-173

Unconventional Warrior

Memoir of a Special Operations Commander in Afghanistan

COLONEL WALTER MORRIS HERD
U.S. ARMY, SPECIAL FORCES (RET.)

McFarland & Company, Inc., Publishers
Jefferson, North Carolina, and London

LIBRARY OF CONGRESS CATALOGUING-IN-PUBLICATION DATA

Herd, Walter M., 1960–
    Unconventional warrior : memoir of a special operations
commander in Afghanistan / Colonel Walter Morris Herd.
        p.   cm.
    Includes index.

    ISBN 978-0-7864-6971-0
    softcover : acid free paper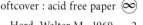

    1. Herd, Walter M., 1960–   2. Afghan War, 2001–
— Commando Operations.   3. Combined Joint Special
Operations Task Force in Afghanistan — Biography.
4. United States. Army. Special Forces — Officers —
Biography.   5. Special forces (Military science) — United
States — Biography.   6. Irregular warfare — United
States — History — 21st century.   7. United States Armed
Forces — Commando troops — History.   8. Afghan War,
2001– — Campaigns.   9. Afghan War, 2001– — Personal
narratives, American.   I. Title.
DS371.43.H48 2013
958.104' 78 — dc23
[B]   2013017769

BRITISH LIBRARY CATALOGUING DATA ARE AVAILABLE

© 2013 Walter Morris Herd. All rights reserved

*No part of this book may be reproduced or transmitted in any form
or by any means, electronic or mechanical, including photocopying
or recording, or by any information storage and retrieval system,
without permission in writing from the publisher.*

Cover photographs: Walter Morris Herd, commander of the
Combined Joint Special Operations Task Force–Afghanistan;
patches, tabs, pins and badges earned by Col. Herd, *top to bottom, left to right:* Master Parachutist Badge; Combat Divers
Badge; Special Forces tab worn by all Green Berets; Ranger tab;
Airborne tab above arrowhead badge are the unit insignia
for US Army Special Forces Command; Combat Infantryman's
Badge; Regimental Crest of the Special Forces Regiment; the
insignia of a colonel on the "flash" of the 3rd Special Forces
Group, worn on the beret; US Army Military Free Fall
qualification wings (all courtesy of the author)

Manufactured in the United States of America

McFarland & Company, Inc., Publishers
   Box 611, Jefferson, North Carolina 28640
   www.mcfarlandpub.com

To fallen comrades I've known over the years.
The price of freedom is high, but the alternative is unaffordable.

MSG Joe Gradzewicz, Special Forces, 27 July 1990
SSG Chad Duvall, Special Forces, 20 January 1996
SSG Joe Suponcic, Special Forces, 15 December 1999 (Kosovo)
1SG Brian Look, Special Forces, 3 March 2001
SSG Paul Sweeney, Special Forces, 30 October 2003 (Afghanistan)
SGT Roy Wood, Special Forces, 10 January 2004 (Afghanistan)
SPC Adam Kinser, PSYOP, 29 January 2004 (Afghanistan)
CW2 Bruce Price, Special Forces, 19 May 2004 (Afghanistan)
CPT Dan Eggers, Special Forces, 29 May 2004 (Afghanistan)
SSG Robert Mogensen, Special Forces, 29 May 2004 (Afghanistan)
PFC Joseph Jeffries, PSYOP, 29 May 2004 (Afghanistan)
BM1 Brian Oullette, SEAL, 29 May 2004 (Afghanistan)

Table of Contents

Preface: Six Generations
of American Patriots

The Young British Soldier
by Rudyard Kipling

When you're wounded and left on Afghanistan's plains,
And the women come out to cut up what remains,
Jest roll to your rifle and blow out your brains
An' go to your Gawd like a soldier.
Go, go, go like a soldier,
Go, go, go like a soldier,
Go, go, go like a soldier,
So-oldier of the Queen!

You can't give a nation its freedom. The people have to earn it in order to respect it and in order to keep it. They have to be part of the process.

Several generations of Americans have been part of the process, including the five that I am following in my family. I am happy to have been part of the process of keeping our nation's freedom, and I hope my story will be an encouragement to the young men and women who now are considering a military career. They will carry on the responsibility of keeping the process alive. I hope also that the veterans who may see this story will find in it many reminders of their service experience, pleasant or not, from my father's generation of World War II patriots, to those patriots of our current wars.

And for those who may have family members or other loved ones entering military service, I trust you will find descriptions that may help you in understanding what they are doing or have done.

But most of all, I pray that the unconventional warfare lessons

1

learned in Afghanistan by fighting "by, with and through" the indigenous people will stay with us in the years to come. We can't solve all the world's problems, of course, nor should we try. But when the opportunity allows, we can often reach our national goals by shifting our efforts to fighting "by, with and through" the locals.

* * *

Twenty years and four months after I moved out of the Beta Theta Pi fraternity house as the Epsilon Chapter president at Centre College in Danville, Kentucky, I took the colors of the Combined Joint Special Operations Task Force to Afghanistan. The unit had 4,000 men and women from seven nations fighting against Muslim extremists in and around Afghanistan. When I took those colors, I was wearing dusty boots and a tan desert-patterned camouflage uniform. I was about 6,000 miles and what seemed like 2,000 years from what I knew in Kentucky. On my head was the field "patrol cap" with the insignia of an Army colonel sewn on the front.

That insignia is an American eagle holding arrows in one talon and olive branches in the other. An American eagle has eyes that can focus in depth, allowing the hunter to view the fields from a thousand feet up and then refocus so that same eagle can swoop down upon its prey with speed, precision and violence, when needed. I had done my best to grow into that eagle, to see as if I were among the mountaintops, but still able to focus with precision when violence was needed.

My command in Afghanistan was the culmination of everything I knew. It took every skill I learned as a child, every value I learned growing up, and every task and theory I learned as a professional soldier to be successful in that command. Every night I prayed the same prayer: "Lord, let me lead these soldiers like they deserve to be led."

When I graduated from Centre College 20 years before I took command in Afghanistan, I was commissioned as a 2nd lieutenant in the Regular Army. When my mother and father pinned on those two 2nd lieutenant bars, one on each shoulder, I became the sixth generation in my family to serve our country.

Those brass bars on my shoulders were originally worn by my father, who earned them during World War II. Dad was in the ROTC

(Reserve Officer Training Corps) at the University of Tennessee, but in 1942, one year prior to his planned graduation, our Army was fully engaged against Nazi Germany. Dad was called up, under the theory that "the Army needs you now, not later." So it was, "Congratulations, Lieutenant, you can finish studying English later; you have a mission to attend to first!"

As a matter of fact, the United States Military Academy at West Point had two classes in 1943: one that graduated in the spring as they normally do, and another that graduated 6 months early, because America needed lieutenants more than college graduates back then. The vast majority of officers then and now were not West Pointers.

As a lieutenant, Dad was an infantry platoon leader in a heavy weapons company of the 84th Infantry Division in Germany. He was wounded shortly before the Germans kicked off the Battle of the Bulge. He spent several months in hospitals in France and England before he was healthy enough to rejoin his unit and link up with his old platoon. That link-up was at the very end of the war. He was told that the officer who had replaced him as platoon leader was killed in the platoon's last firefight of the war. My father told me he thought the Lord was looking over him several times and that the day he was wounded was the luckiest day of his life because it allowed him to survive the war. I am sure the Nazi soldier who pulled the trigger was not aiming to make my father a lucky man.

I was commissioned in 1983, almost exactly 40 years after my father. Dad was surprised that I wasn't commissioned as an infantry officer, because in his day it seemed that almost every new lieutenant had been commissioned as an infantry officer. In 1943 that's the way it was; that was the greatest need in our Army. "If you've got two good feet then you're in the infantry." You may end up shooting a cannon but normally infantry was where you first were assigned during World War II. But I was commissioned as an artillery officer in 1983.

I feel a tie with my father and I've enjoyed looking at the historical differences between his army and my army. I asked him once how they planned for big operations during his day. He said, "I don't really remember being involved in any detailed planning. I do remember one time as we were just crossing into Germany there was one regiment on the left and one regiment on the right and my platoon was in the middle. Everybody was to shoot everything that they had at that village and then start walking." And that was the plan.

I look now at how detailed our plans are, all the way down to the squad level, so that everybody understands the complete tactical situation: the commander's intent; the contingency plans; if something goes right or wrong with branches and sequence; the entire leadership chain. If the commander is killed, who moves up and takes command? When does the main effort shift from Alpha company to Bravo company? Yet back in 1944 and 1945 it seemed to be: "You're on the left, I'm on the right and we're shooting at that village! Let's go."

Sometimes the KISS principle is the best answer after all: "Keep it simple, stupid!" You don't have to be perfect: you just have to be better than your opponent. In 1944 and '45 we were better than any opponent, and that's all that mattered.

I was very lucky: I never was wounded.—A wound is something inflicted by the enemy. I was shot at several times, but never hit. I like to think God had other plans for me. I had a few minor injuries, lots of bumps and bruises, a couple of parachute jumps that rang my bell pretty hard, my ankles and knees are torn up and I had an infection that almost took my leg, but I was never wounded.

For generations back my family all answered the call. My mother flew observation patrols in a small Piper Cub for the Civil Air Patrol. She learned to fly at the University of Tennessee, where she was a student, as part of an experimental program to see if women could fly airplanes. She and a few other volunteer co-eds flew these "recon missions" around seemingly unimportant small towns near Knoxville. One of these small towns was Oak Ridge, Tennessee. Unbeknownst to her and her peers, they were working on the Manhattan Project in Oak Ridge, building the first atomic bomb. Our family likes to think it was because of her air reconnaissance flights that the Germans never made it as far as Tennessee!

My grandfather, Walter Lee Morris, for whom I am named, served during World War I in the U.S. Navy. One of his bunkmates was a young Norman Rockwell. I have the Bible my grandfather carried with him during the "war to end all wars." It contains a note written to him from his father that says if you read this book and take the lessons to heart, you will be greatly blessed. "Read, read, read," is how the inscription ends. That was good advice to a young man going to war in 1917, as well as now, and I have tried to follow it all of my life.

My father's grandfather, my great-grandfather, Felix Motlow (for whom my father, Charles Felix Herd, is named) was a Confederate infantryman in the Civil War. He served in the 1st Tennessee Volunteer Regiment. He joined that regiment when it was first formed and he was very young, shortly after Confederate Colonel Pierre Gustave Toutant Beauregard opened fire on Ft. Sumter, South Carolina, in April 1861. The 1st Tennessee served in the Army of Northern Virginia. They charged across the field at Gettysburg with General Pickett.

One of the battles in which they fought was at Cedar Mountain, near Culpeper in Virginia. By coincidence, I fox hunted around Cedar Mountain as a young captain with the Bull Run Hunt club while I was stationed in Washington, D.C., on my first of two tours there. I am certain I had more fun galloping my thoroughbred down trails and over jumps on Cedar Mountain than my great-grandfather did dodging Minié balls while wearing threadbare britches.

At the end of the war, my great-grandfather was one of just seven of the original volunteers in his company who were able to walk back to Tennessee from Appomattox Court House, Virginia, after General Lee surrendered on April 9, 1865.

His grandfather, Lt. John Motlow, served in the American Revolutionary War. After the war, Lt. Motlow was one of two survivors in his family of an Indian massacre. One afternoon, Lt. Motlow, his parents, and his sister Mary were on a carriage ride when they were stopped by a band of renegade Indians led by a surviving British mercenary named Bloody Bart.

During the war, the British had hired various mercenaries to get the Indians riled up enough to fight against the patriots. This was how the tradition of scalping gained notoriety in North America. The British would pay the Indians for each scalp in order to encourage them to carry the fight to the patriots. After the war, some of those mercenaries and some of those Indians still found it profitable to rob the patriots, with the occasional scalping included. Well, Bloody Bart and his Indians were just such people. They ambushed and killed Lt. Motlow's parents and scalped Mary Motlow (for whom my sister Mary Motlow Herd Jackson is named) and left her for dead. She apparently had red hair and Bloody Bart and his Indians thought that color unique. She survived, but she went through the rest of her life scalped and wearing a bonnet.

Lt. John Motlow was the next to go. The Indians tied him up. They were about to kill him when Bloody Bart said something like, "Wait a minute. Before you kill him, take off his boots." As they were pulling off his boots, Motlow kicked free and he ran through the night for all he was worth — probably one boot on and one boot off — with the Indians after him. He hid in the overhang of a creek (appropriately now named Motlow Creek, near their property in the Carolinas). The Indians continued searching, but ran by his hiding place and he never saw them again.

Our family legend recalls that over time, Motlow grew into a highly respected man in his small rural community. A few years after the family tragedy, Motlow found out that Bloody Bart had been arrested in a nearby village for stealing horses. So Motlow went to the county magistrate and asked him to release Bloody Bart on Motlow's recognizance. The magistrate obliged. Motlow then gave Bloody Bart a minute or so to make peace with his Maker before shooting him in the middle of the street. Motlow immediately stepped into the stirrups of his horse and rode to Tennessee to take control of the land grant property he had been given for his service in the war. And that's how our family became Tennesseans about 200 years ago. That same farm is where my grandmother grew up.

My family history takes us all the way back to John Motlow's father — also John Motlow — who served in the colonial militia under Colonel William Eason, Granville County, North Carolina, in 1754, during the French and Indian War. When the alarm was sounded, he and his neighbors ran with their muskets to the action.

Those are the six generations in my family who have served their nation. I expect there will be more in the future.

As I tell veterans everywhere, "American veterans all signed a blank check payable to your nation." Luckily no one in my family had to cash that check in full, and none of my ancestors was killed in the line of duty. Sure, all of those checks have been cashed to some extent, with blood, sweat and tears, but not with death.

Preface

Like some professions, soldiering seems to be a family profession. Today, less than one half of one percent of America's citizens are in uniform, yet half of the soldiers in our Army have family members who served. That means we are going back to the same families generation after generation, asking for their service and sacrifice. When I am invited to talk on patriotic or military subjects I tell groups that if they cannot reach out and touch someone in their family who has worn a uniform or at least risked death on the line in some way or another, that family has not been living up to its part. Freedom is not kept with our tax dollars alone; it is kept with our time, blood, sweat and tears.

1

The Making of an Unconventional Warrior

After a family history of some 175 years in Tennessee, my immediate family was the first to move away when my father resigned as the chief executive officer of the Chamber of Commerce in Knoxville to accept the CEO position with the Chamber in Louisville, Kentucky.

I was just beginning the first grade. As a kid growing up in the '60s and '70s in the suburbs of Louisville, I did what every young kid in those years did: I played imaginary games of "cowboys and Indians."

I also played a lot of "army" in the woods of our suburban area. I dug trenches and small bunkers for my plastic toy soldiers all throughout our back yard. These toy soldiers had primary and alternate fighting positions, communications trenches and pillboxes for their recoilless rifles. I even stretched small coils of (what looked to me like) barbed wire in front of their positions. Recently, after more than 40 years, my father found a few of these soldiers while he was replanting an old flower bed. These soldiers were still in position, still ready to go ... and probably in better shape than I!

When I grew up, my brother and I both played varsity football at Ballard High School in Louisville. I had a great time. I was never too far from the line of scrimmage. I played center on offense and middle linebacker on defense. Like all football players, I learned how to hit and get hit. I learned how to play when I was tired or hurt — all good skills for a future soldier to have.

I was very involved in Boy Scouts and became an Eagle Scout shortly after my older brother, Charles Jr., earned his Eagle Scout rank. On one of my early scout campouts we were tested on our ability to build a fire.

We had three matches to get a fire going, using only leaves and twigs that we found around our campsite. I'd like to say that it was the rain and wet wood, but I expect I just did not know how to build a proper fire. I simply could not get that thing going. The scout master said, "Not burning — you fail. Try again next week." Honest feedback, clear standards. You can bet that I became an ace fire builder after that.

On another scout campout, I was given an "Ordeal" test. In this test, we had to work all day with little food and no conversation and then sleep alone in the woods. What great training for a young soldier-to-be! I loved physical team activity. I loved walking through the woods. I loved doing the kinds of things that future soldiers enjoy.

So it was no big surprise, I guess, that when I went to Centre College in Danville, Kentucky, I took a class in ROTC. Centre is a small liberal arts college in the center of the Bluegrass state. It has consistently ranked highly in most of the college rating polls. Good students and great faculty produce loyal alumni. I really enjoyed Centre and my first ROTC classes. So I took more ROTC classes. I really liked those as well. I went to ROTC basic camp the summer between my freshman and sophomore years and then advanced camp the following summer.

I was ultimately commissioned a 2nd lieutenant when I graduated from Centre with a bachelor's degree in history and a minor in education. Many folks study history; I got a chance to see some of it and even to add a small footnote to it. Most of the students at Centre go on to medical school or law school. Many work for their parents in a family business. I was one of the very few who went to work for my Uncle Sam, in our family business— the United States Army.

2

Initial Training

After college, I went through the officers' basic course at Ft. Sill, Oklahoma, where I learned the specifics of being an artilleryman. Pulling the lanyard on an 8-inch howitzer really makes the earth move under your feet.

I went to Ranger school after the artillery officers' basic course because I knew that I wanted to push the envelope a bit more. In the two months of Ranger training, I lost 20 pounds even though I started off in the best shape of my life. I weighed about 170 pounds; I could do push-ups, sit-ups, pull-ups and run, it seemed, all day long.

Ranger school is really a training event where you learn how to *lead*. But the classroom is the great outdoors. You learn patrolling, land navigation and small unit tactics. You patrol in the desert, in the mountains, and in the swamps. You do it in whatever weather the good Lord passes your way. You learn how far you can push yourself and your fellow Rangers. If you can lead soldiers after days without sleep and just one meal a day for the past week, then you can really lead soldiers. Ranger school was like an August football practice that never ends. It was what I'd been getting ready for since I could walk.

I am a "winter Ranger," meaning that I went through the training in the winter. My class began in February 1984 and graduated in early April. Much of the school is at Ft. Benning, Georgia, and takes about two months. The cold makes everything more difficult. One night was colder than I ever thought Georgia could be. Ranger students are always paired up in two-man teams. In cold weather, every two men share one poncho liner, a nylon blanket-like device that can be tied into a poncho for warmth. My Ranger buddy was Nasty Nealson. He was a private in the first Ranger Battalion in Savannah, the battalion I would later join as a first lieutenant. He was called "Nasty" because he always had a mouth full of tobacco with constant streams of brown tobacco juice running down his chin. After days without shaving, washing or even brushing his teeth he was—well, nasty.

One night he and I were in the field on the perimeter of our small patrol base in the mountains outside of Dahlonega, Georgia. We'd just finished our guard shift so we leaned up against our two rucksacks and pulled our poncho liner over our legs and got some sleep. When we woke up about two hours later, we realized that our canteens were frozen solid. These canteens had been strapped on to our bodies and we were under a blanket, and *still* the temperature was cold enough to freeze the water. I vowed that I would never take off my long underwear again (thin and worn as it was). Of course, I rethought that vow when we landed in Florida three weeks later for our jungle phase of training.

Our final phase of Ranger training was jungle training. I remember being so tired that I actually looked forward to our parachute jump into the training area. As we jumped into Eglin Air Force Base in the panhandle of Florida, I realized with great joy that I would have about 45 seconds of peaceful bliss while under the parachute canopy. After we jumped out of the C-130 Hercules airplane about 1200 feet above the ground and before I landed like a bag of rocks, I got to rest for 45 precious seconds. That is tired!

The last day of training was a final raid against an objective just inland from the coast. We paddled several hundred meters in our rubber, eight-man Zodiac inflatable boats, then carried the boat off the beach and patrolled several kilometers inland to the raid objective. After that, with what little energy we had left, we began our long march back to the Florida Ranger camp. I think that was the most painful twelve miles I have ever walked. Heavy rucksacks full of ammunition and supplies, blisters on every part of my body aggravated from the salt and sand. The silver lining was being in the company of great Americans!

Two days later we were in formation on Ranger Field at Ft. Benning, Georgia. My future wife, Ann, pinned the black and gold Ranger Tab on the top of my left sleeve. My parents looked on thankfully.

3

First Assignment

Unfortunately, being a Ranger doesn't necessarily mean you join a Ranger battalion, and I didn't at first. Instead, as a young 2nd lieutenant right out of Ranger School, I reported to 24th Infantry Division at Ft. Stewart, Georgia. My first day in the office, I walked in wearing my class A uniform and reported to my commander, Captain Andy Douglass, just like I'd been taught: "Lt. Herd reporting for duty, Sir."

"Great, Herd," he said. "Come with me." He immediately led me to the arms room — or the "weapons storage room" — where I proceeded to inventory something like 165 or so M-16s, a handful of pistols, bayonets, and so on. There I was in my nice new class A uniform with brand new shiny jump wings and 2nd lieutenant bars, reading off the serial numbers of each weapon as CPT Douglass checked the numbers against the hand receipt to ensure that all were present. I get a kick out of that when I think back on it. I think CPT Douglass was pulling my chain a little bit as well.

I'll never forget a big division exercise we had at Ft. Stewart. The entire 24th Infantry Division was out on this one. Our division commander was MG "Stormin' Norman" Schwarzkopf, later of Desert Storm fame. I was leading my platoon from one side of the fort to the other on a large, motorized tactical convoy movement at night. There happens to be a Georgia state highway that runs through the middle of the fort, so to make sure that none of my soldiers was hit by a tractor trailer or some other civilian vehicle, we had to stop and make an *administrative* crossing of that highway. Our plan was that as we approached the highway from our sandy tank trails, we would put flashing lights on both sides of the road and place road guards out there to alert any civilian drivers that two dozen armored vehicles were about to cross the highway.

Then we switched our headlights from "black-out drive" to regular headlights and crossed the road one vehicle at a time until everyone was safely on the other side and back on the sand tank trail. With 30 or so sleepy soldiers in their tracked vehicles, I wanted to manage the actual crossing myself, because at night, almost everything is "high risk" and the best way to mitigate that risk is for leaders to be present at the event.

So, I told my guys to cross and then to stop on the other side of the highway and wait for me. The plan was that I would be the last one to cross and I would signal the first one in line to follow me. Well, it happened that the first one of my vehicles to cross the highway was a self-propelled eight-inch howitzer, an M-110. The 8-inch (203 mm) M-110 Self-Propelled Howitzer was the largest *self-propelled howitzer* we had in the *United States Army*'s inventory at the time. It was deployed in the division's artillery brigade, called "DIVARTY," in general support battalions to conduct general support, *counterbattery fire* missions for the division's missions. My battalion commander called these weapons "city levelers" because of their size and firepower.

That first howitzer in line that night crossed the road and just kept going. He kept going and kept going, into the darkness. I eventually crossed the road with the rest of the platoon and chased him across post for the next two or three hours. I finally got up to him and yelled from my little M-151 Jeep in the middle of the night, "Who are you following? I told you to wait and follow me!" He said, "I thought I was following you, sir!" Apparently, he followed someone else in a Jeep because all Jeeps pretty much look the same at 2:00 or 3:00 o'clock in the morning.

4

Transfer to the Rangers

It was on Ft. Stewart that I had another bean-counting session like I did with CPT Douglass, although this one was with considerably less humor. I got a call one night after I had gotten home from the battalion area to my two-bedroom apartment in Hinesville, Georgia. The call was from the Battalion Motor Officer saying that I had to come back to the motor pool. "Why? What's the problem?" I asked.

"The battalion commander is down here and he wants you to fix some things on one of your vehicles," he replied.

"Well, exactly what's the problem?"

"One of your taillights is out on one of the trailers," he said.

"Okay. I got it. No problem," I said. "I'll get to it in the morning. Surely, that's not something you have to do in the middle of the night."

I lost the argument. I went down there and, sure enough, the battalion commander was there with virtually every lieutenant in the battalion going from vehicle to vehicle checking things like taillights, oil levels and that sort of thing. Lo and behold, one of my ammunition trailers had a taillight out, so I replaced the light bulb. It quickly dawned on me that this part of the Army was not the place I needed to spend the rest of my life.

I began to work on a plan to leave the 24th Infantry Division, Ft. Stewart, Georgia and go up the road to Savannah, Georgia, about forty-five minutes away, and Hunter Army Air Field, where the First Ranger Battalion was headquartered. The First Ranger Battalion, or 1st of the 75th Infantry (Ranger), consists of the best light infantry in the world. It is one of the three Ranger battalions in the Army — the 1st at Hunter Army Air Field in Savannah, Georgia; the 2nd at Ft. Lewis, Washington; and the 3rd at Ft. Benning, Georgia.

I made some calls. While I was one of only two Ranger-qualified officers in my artillery battalion in the 24th, in the Ranger Battalions every officer and NCO, as well as most of the younger soldiers, were qualified to wear the black and gold Ranger tab that my wife had pinned on my shoulder a year earlier.

The 1st of the 75th happened to have an opening for an artillery lieutenant as a fire support officer. I went to Hunter Army Air Field and was interviewed by the Ranger battalion commander. After I made a few more calls, I asked my battalion commander at Ft. Stewart if I could go. My boss at Ft. Stewart said, "Herd, you can't go until I get a replacement for you. Go find me another lieutenant to take your place here in my battalion at Ft Stewart."

He came back to me a couple of weeks later and said, "Okay, Herd, no problem. I got your replacement. I got a new lieutenant that's going to come next week and replace you."

I took a set of orders out of my desk and said, "Thank you, sir. Here are my orders. I report there Monday morning."

I'll never forget the look on his face, fiery red with smoke coming from his ears. When I first met him several months prior, he had pulled on the Ranger tab sewn onto my left shoulder and said something like, "What a waste of time. I could teach you more about soldiering in a two-week field training exercise here at Ft. Stewart."

He further endeared himself to me one morning during PT (physical training) when I had my platoon doing exercises before a long run around the post. Rather than showing an interest in the quality of the workout, he focused on several soldiers who were out of step with each other while doing pushups. Attention to detail is only valuable if you are paying attention to the right details.

While in the Rangers, we did an exercise in Honduras that I later learned was what senior officers call a *show of force* exercise. The whole battalion parachuted into a jungle drop zone about five kilometers from the Honduran-Nicaraguan border. In 45 seconds, the small field changed from being a sleepy place for lizards to sun themselves to an assembly area for a battalion of the world's best trained killers.

I remember one time during that deployment we went out on a mortar firing point in the jungle. There was a Honduran lieutenant with us. I said, "Okay, lieutenant, what are our left and right limits? Where out here can we safely fire our mortars?"

He pointed to one tree and said in English, "Okay, that tree is your left limit."

Then he made a complete circle, came back to that same tree and said, "That tree is your right limit. You can shoot anywhere you want in any direction." They had an interesting perspective on weapon safety. So we shot our 60 MM mortars there for a couple of hours.

Soon, I saw some people downrange of where we were shooting, some local Indians, and I called, "Cease fire! Cease fire! Clear your weapons!"

I called this Honduran lieutenant back and said, "Hey, there are people down there — there are native Indians down there where we're shooting! What do you want to do?"

So he simply looked out over the hill and yelled, I assume in the local dialect, not in Spanish, something like, "Go away. We're shooting."

Then he turned back to me and said, "All right. Continue shooting."

Again, an interesting perspective on safety. I took it upon myself to make sure there was no chance of any people being in harm's way.

That tour in the First Ranger Battalion was probably one of those definitive periods in my career. I absolutely loved it. One night on the Honduran-Nicaraguan border in 1986, I looked around and said to myself, "You know, I've been in the Army three years. My commitment's up. I can get out now anytime I want." But I realized then and there that I was in the company of heroes. I was on an all-star team with those young Rangers right there on the cutting edge of democracy, on the Honduran-Nicaraguan border. I loved it.

5

Airborne!

Many of the aches and pains soldiers like me collect over the years are due to being a paratrooper. To become a paratrooper in our Army you first must go to a three-week airborne school in Ft. Benning, Georgia. I went to Airborne school as a 2nd lieutenant, right before I started Ranger training. The three weeks are broken down into *ground week*, when you learn the techniques of hitting the ground; then *tower week*, when you learn the techniques of exiting the aircraft and flying the parachute to the ground — you do that generally off a 250-foot tower — and then *jump week*, when you put it all together and jump out of an airplane five times, 3 day and 2 night jumps. The airborne motto is ALL THE WAY! That is how far the paratrooper will go to succeed with the mission: all the way.

Later on when I was in the First Ranger Battalion I went to Jumpmaster School as a 1st lieutenant. At Jumpmaster School, you learn not only how to jump, but you learn how to manage and lead all types of airborne operations, how to inspect fellow jumpers, how to inspect airplanes, and how to run the entire operation, which is much more complicated than just preparing your own body for exit from the airplane.

Before every jump, there's something called sustained airborne training, or SAT, which is simply a refresher on what to do in every possible contingency; it's very regimented and very much built into the culture, and it's very specific to the environment of the immediate jump. I have given and received sustained airborne training in just about every environment you can jump into. I've received it for a snow jump in Canada, a desert jump in Texas, and a jump into the jungles of the Honduras. Any time I was jumping out of a military airplane, all the jumpers would get together and the jumpmaster would give a review. And that

18

review was very deliberate; it would walk you through everything that could possibly go wrong, and then you would repeat it so it was on the tip of your tongue.

The five points of performance are: *exit the aircraft; tight body position and count; look out for fellow jumpers; prepare to land;* and finally, *land.* And you rehearse those and you practice them and you get in that body position with your feet and knees together, toes pointed down, knees slightly bent so that you hit the balls of your feet, your calves, your buttocks, your push-up muscles and your back.

There are two emergency landing drills that may be reviewed again in sustained airborne training: one is water landing and the other is a tree landing. Depending on where you jump, you may or may not go over any of those. For example, when I jumped in some desert exercises out west, we didn't rehearse any water contingency because there was no water within 100 miles of our DZ. But if there's any water near the DZ, it's intense. If you're missing the drop zone and going toward a lake you have to take different actions than if you're missing the drop zone and going toward a forest.

If you're heading for the water, you want to disconnect the chest strap and the waist strap with the reserve attached right before you land. As soon as you hit the water, you disconnect the leg straps so that you can swim out of your parachute. That's for an unscheduled water landing.

In an emergency tree landing, you do the opposite. You keep your reserve parachute in front of you to protect your body from possible injury from branches or limbs. You keep everything buckled up and you cover your face and body with your arms so you don't get poked in the eye, and then you prepare to land as normal so if you do go through the branches, you still land properly. I've done several planned water jumps, meaning I didn't have to cut away my parachute because I had a buoyancy compensator.

I did one unplanned tree landing. I got out of the airplane late because I was the last man on a short drop zone. We had already overflown the end of the drop zone when I exited the bird one night. When I got out I looked down toward the drop zone — basically a large field — but it was about a quarter of a mile behind me. As soon as I got under the canopy, I looked at the airplane and looked at the parachute to make sure it had no holes. I gained my canopy control and looked at the ground and realized that the drop zone was out of my reach.

So I started looking around — at night — for something that looked like the softest place to land. There was a patch of small pine trees, a small patch about thirty or forty feet wide. I did what I'd been trained to do: I went right through them, I kept my feet together so I wouldn't have a branch go between my legs, I covered my face so I wouldn't get slapped with a branch and I prepared to land in case I went all the way through.

Unfortunately, I was stuck.

If you get suspended in the air between the top of the tree and the ground, you have to pull your ripcord so your reserve pops out of your reserve parachute harness and dangles down toward the ground and then climb down the reserve, which is basically like thirty feet of ropes and nylon, to the ground. I was suspended between the top of the tree and ground.

That emergency tree landing turned out to be one of the softest I ever had! I was able to simply unsnap my kit and hop two feet out and bounce to the ground — pretty easy. One of my friends was suspended way up in the air in another tree and he had to lower himself all the way down on the reserve parachute. I got lucky. I'd rather be lucky than good any day — and I got lucky a lot.

6

Jumpmaster

I went to jumpmaster school while I was in the 1st Ranger Battalion and had a great time there. The school itself is about two weeks long. The jumpmaster training takes an ordinary paratrooper with about 20 jumps under his or her belt and teaches them the true science behind the process of parachuting soldiers. A jumpmaster must know every part of the parachute and the jump platform and how to identify and articulate a problem.

I remember a few months after I graduated, I was the jumpmaster for a nighttime airborne operation. I was supposed to hang out the door of a C130 flying about 750 feet above the ground on a battalion mass tack as we jumped in on an airfield at Ft. Bragg, North Carolina. Now a *battalion mass tack* means that the entire Ranger battalion, some 650 men, are under parachute canopy at the same time. We had about eight C130s, each full of paratroopers ready for action.

That night we were doing something called a CARP, a computed air release point. That means that the pilots compute when to turn the green lights on because it's pitch black on the ground and the jumpmaster can't see any of the known points on the ground while he or she is looking out of the door.

I had studied this during the JM training, of course, and had done several CARP jumps as a jumper, but never as a jumpmaster until that night over Ft. Bragg. The Air Force load master in the back of the airplane gave us the two-minute warning and opened the jump door. I checked the door to make sure it was opened properly, and then I leaned out as far as I could to look for the drop zone because that's what you're supposed to do as a jumpmaster. And I realized, "It's pitch black!" I couldn't see a darn thing. We could be jumping into the Atlantic Ocean for all I could see.

However, I had total faith in the Air Force C130 pilots. I came back in and gave the jumpers a two-minute, a one-minute and a thirty-second warning. The light turned green and out we went into the darkness. Thank goodness when we hit the ground, we were right where we were supposed to be. In about 60 seconds, that drop zone at Ft. Bragg went from a silent empty field, to one filled with a battalion of the world's best infantrymen: American Rangers.

7

A Lesson in Leadership

The battalion commander for the 1st Rangers, Lt. Col. Keith Knight, taught me a lot about leading soldiers. Maybe he didn't realize he did it, but he did. He gave the officers a lecture one time that really rang true to young Lt. Herd. He said, "Each one of you is successful in this battalion because of your ability to manage in extreme detail what's going on. Each one of you, however, will fail as you move up through the ranks if you don't quit managing in extreme detail and begin to manage and shape the big picture."

That hit home because the higher you get in rank the more you need to focus not only on the details but on the big picture. That's where military operations typically go wrong: misunderstanding the big picture. Wars are seldom lost because of details, but they often are lost because leaders did not read the big picture correctly. The Germans did not lose in Russia during World War II because of a poor performance of the Panzer regiments; they lost because Hitler did not understand the holistic environment of Russia.

Army officers are really part artist and part scientist. Napoleon, for example, was a master of the science of ballistics and the science of logistics. He knew how many tons of grain a cavalry division needed to ride 50 miles. He said that amateurs argue over tactics but professionals argue over logistics.

He also was skilled in the art of fighting with a corps. The reason Napoleon ruled much of Europe was that he was the only military commander who could maneuver entire corps, hundreds of thousands of men. Everybody else maneuvered smaller divisions, but Napoleon understood the special art of moving corps around the battlefield.

Now, part of that art, of course, is the *art of leadership*. There have

23

been thousands of books written about leadership. The theory I use, the theory I've tried to train my younger officers on, and certainly the theory that I've practiced over the years, is that *leadership is like golf.*

I don't play golf myself. Golf takes patience and time. I have very little time and virtually no patience. But I've seen it on TV. I think I've learned the point.

Clearly there are three tasks at which you need to excel to win at golf, and I believe these are the same three tasks that a good leader needs to master.

The first task is situational awareness. When you step up to the tee, you need to understand how the course flows. You need to understand that you have a 200-meter green that slopes off to the right with trees on the left and water down at the bottom and it doglegs just a little bit to the left. You have to think consequences and next steps, too. Unless you hit a hole-in-one, you have to think about setting up the second shot. This is situational awareness, or SA: you have to "see" all of these things as you sweep the course with your eyes—where you are, where you want to be, and how best to get there. You need to have situational awareness to master your first task in golf.

The second task is to choose the right club. Based on the lay of the land, plus the wind; based on the type of soil; based on the distance you want the ball to go, and whether you need to shoot straight and low, or high and over something, you choose a specific type of club.

The third task is to properly use that club. You have to have your fingers interlaced just right, your elbows locked, your eye on the ball, knees flexed, hips bent and follow through with your eyes.

It takes mastering all three of those tasks to play a good game.

The same three skills are needed in leadership. You have to understand the situation. You've need to choose the right club—in this case the right course of action—and you have to use the club properly. Three tasks: situational awareness, the right course of action, and proper execution of that option.

A good leader has a bag full of techniques and a variety of leadership styles to use on a personal level or on the operational level. A good leader can yell and scream, or coach and mentor. Maybe the club to pull is empathy—offer a shoulder to a sad or pained soldier and help him or her through the day. The point is, after tasks #1 and #2, a good leader needs to use that leadership tool properly.

I believe that the biggest errors in leadership are found in the first task, situational awareness, in misunderstanding the situation. If you don't get this right, the next two steps won't matter. Let's say I'm leading a patrol and it gets a bit tense to the point where every 100 yards is important. If I misunderstand the situation, if I don't notice something that's out of place — maybe an out-of-place motion or a shadow where it ought not to be, maybe a fraction of a tire impression where it shouldn't be — if my SA is low, I might get my soldiers in trouble.

That's one of the biggest problems with leadership — misunderstanding the situation. When you mistakenly think the situation is one way, you choose an option and execute that option properly, only to realize that you misread the situation and you had the wrong option to begin with. Or you stay too one-dimensional and don't consider the effect of your action in terms of the next effects.

One of the truisms in military history is that good tactics can't save a bad strategy. That was true for both Hitler and Napoleon when they invaded Russia. They had great soldiers, great generals, and great tactics. But they both were following an inherently flawed strategy. They both lost, consequently, in the same manner. Unfortunately, that same truism can be true for the United State, too.

8

Time to Move On

After about two years in the 1st Ranger Battalion, I was promoted to captain. Unfortunately, I also knew it was time to move on in the Army. It was time for me to PCS. PCS means *permanent change of station,* though after several permanent changes of station, I realized it's really only a *temporary* change of station. I PCS'd about 14 times in 24 years. For all practical purposes, it was time for me to PCS from Hunter Army Air Field Base back into the conventional Army. I left the Rangers and attended the artillery advanced course back at Ft. Sill, Oklahoma, because that's what young artillery captains do.

One of the classes we had was nuclear targeting. I'll never forget the instructor. He was a pale-faced, pasty-skinned, chubby captain. He was almost the personification of what you would expect of a geek. He probably had a slide rule and a pocket protector — that sort of guy. About halfway through that class I realized I needed to get out of the artillery. Remember now, I was just coming from the 1st Ranger Battalion, where the weakest guy there was still a stud. I had just rotated back into the conventional Army but I really missed that airborne Special Operations culture.

Having just left the Rangers, I was in great physical shape and I intended to stay that way for the six months of the artillery course. Every morning before class I met with the younger lieutenants who wanted to go to the Ranger School after their Artillery Officers Basic Course, and we worked out. All of us got in great shape. I also spent about three nights a week practicing kempo karate in the local dojo. A "dojo" is a martial arts studio.

Our master taught us that there are really three levels of mastering karate: to harm yourself (by accident, of course), to harm your opponent, and to control the amount of harm you do at all. I mastered the first level, became somewhat proficient in the second, and never got close to the third.

There was only one viable option for me to get out of the conventional Army and that was to go to this brand new branch called Special Forces (SF).

The Army has had Special Forces since the early 1950s when the 10th Special Forces Group originally stood up. But it only became a branch while I was in the artillery advanced course. Being its own *branch* meant that SF officers could have their own career track for promotions and assignments. They would no longer have to clear the assignment gates in two areas, like Artillery *and* Special Forces. Being a branch of the Army allowed SF officers to focus their entire career on the art and science of being an unconventional warrior. I saw this as a huge step in the right direction.

9

Understanding Special Operations Structure

U.S. Special Operations Command (USSOCOM) is a combatant command, like U.S. European Command, Central Command, Southern Command, and a few other major American war-fighting commands. The commander is a four-star general and the command rotates between services: Army, Navy and Air Force, every two or three years. The headquarters (HQ) is in Tampa, at McDill Air Force Base.

Each of the services (Army, Navy, Air Force and Marines) has a component or an element — a subordinate unit — in USSOCOM. And every one of those component commanders works for the USSOCOM commanding general. SOCOM is funded by Congress, like Congress funds the services (Army, Navy, Air Force and Marines). That is, Congress funds the Army, Navy, Air Force, Marines *and* SOCOM. So SOCOM gets some of its funding from their services and some from Congress. For example, the Army paid my salary but SOCOM paid for my special training and any special weapons. If I were an artillery or conventional infantry officer the Army would pay for my salary, weapons and all the training.

SOCOM was first stood up via the Nunn-Cohen Act in 1987. That act established SOCOM to protect Special Operations from being smothered by the services. The services, the Army in particular, had never taken care of or appreciated Special Ops, as was evident by the lack of funds and promotions for Special Operations forces and people.

So with the Nunn-Cohen Act, Congress funded USSOCOM as a line item, like a free-standing military. And that made the command come to life.

SOCOM is basically broken down into about two major tasks, and several supporting ones. One task is unconventional warfare (UW)—working *by, with and through* surrogate forces. SOCOM is the only DOD asset tasked and organized to fight this kind of war. The other SOCOM task is surgically precise, extremely violent, direct-action (DA) raids. These latter operations are unilateral, U.S. military against the enemy, precision kill. These could be overt or covert. It simply means that it's paid, funded and executed by the U.S. military, as opposed to a combined Unconventional Warfare mission that originates with us but is done *by, with and through* others. These are the two missions of SOCOM. You work through the locals or you do the sort of dramatic stuff you see in the movies.

Both UW and DA are extremely challenging; both can be extremely dangerous; both are critical to achieving specific ends and our national objectives. Every soldier, sailor or airman in USSOCOM is assessed, recruited, trained and funded to do *or at least support* one of those two missions. They have different organizations, different personalities, different ways of thinking, different equipment for these different missions. It is either the *by, with and through* unconventional task or the direct-action, unilateral, precision-raid task.

Coincidentally, a lot of the personality traits required for the two different missions are the same, so a lot of the people cross back and forth over the course of a career, just as some great athletes play two sports. There are some similar skills used in both track and football, but they are totally different games.

As I grew up as a Ranger our task was very simple to understand—strike, kill, destroy, return. That's it. All unilateral. I never had anybody other than a U.S. service member on my left or right. Our job was to gather intelligence, go in quickly, be violent, kill who needs to be killed, and return.

Once I moved on to Special Forces, though, I went to the other side, to the "dark side" as we called it, where the main effort is not to put six hundred American soldiers on an airfield and kill everybody before sunrise but rather to work with a dozen Americans and maybe 600 locals to do the same things, with our elements usually having invisible fingerprints. The assessment program and the training program in the organizational structure is different for those two missions—direct action or unconventional warfare — but we often have the same objectives and we often need the same skill sets from our people.

Navy Special Operations Command: The SEALs are well known and part of contemporary culture. Let's look at them as an example. NAVSOC, Navy Special Operations Command, is commanded by a three-star admiral. NAVSOC consists mainly of SEALs and special boat units as the delivery mechanisms for SEALs.

The SEALS are broken down into a couple of components. They have SEALs that work for the conventional Navy in the fleet. They're called "fleet SEALs." Each aircraft carrier or battle group that sails around the world has a platoon or so of SEALS on them so that they can do precise, unilateral, violent, surgical operations if need be. Here's an example: if they're sailing through the Suez Canal and there is a hostage scenario or an embassy that needs help, or some pirates that have taken hostages, they have a platoon of SEALs right there who can take care of it. These fleet SEALs "walk softly and carry a big stick," as President Teddy Roosevelt said of our great white fleet in 1908. Amen.

The other category of SEALs are in the SEALs teams that we read about in the media, the SEALs that do predominantly unilateral missions in support of national objectives. A SEAL team is commanded by a SEAL captain (Navy equivalent to an Army colonel). It has three SEAL platoons each commanded by a commander (Army lt. col. equivalent). I've worked with them through several training exercises, and I had a platoon of SEALs working for me in Afghanistan. They did great jobs on their unilateral reconnaissance missions and a few direct action raids as well. In Afghanistan, the SEALs gave me a fast unilateral capability right there within my command. I had two platoons that rotated in and out every 4 to 6 months. These platoons came from both the west coast and east coast. While they both are in the Navy, east and west coasters sometimes consider themselves as different as night and day. I think of them as SEALs. I didn't think of them as a member of a particular SEAL team. All SEALs, all great American patriots and warriors. In 24 years of service, I never met a SEAL that I did not personally like and respect; they are just great guys — and their capabilities are astonishing. As we see in the news, SEAL teams do some great work for the cause of freedom. Yes, they had some great intelligence grown from a decade of building a network made up of multiple indigenous sources, but the SEALs are resourced and trained for that mission. Killing Osama Bin Laden was a great day for America.

The SEALs, the individual sailors, frequently go from each of those elements back and forth. They'll do a year or two of fleet, three or four years in one SEAL team, three or four years in another SEAL team, and then somewhere else as they progress and rotate around. Typically they all start in very young, right off the street, and go to BUDS, Basic Underwater Demolition, which is the basic SEAL qualification course. They also go to some Army schools, including jump school at Ft. Benning, and sometimes other Army schools as well. But as you might expect, they're very physical and they're very comfortable in the water; that's really their forte. So when you need extreme strength, extreme energy and extreme "hit 'em hard capability," in my command that was a force to call upon, and I did. They lived in my headquarters at Bagram Air Base, in their own little sub-compound within my compound. We all ate in the same mess hall, which was a Special Ops mess hall. We had the same motor pool. We shared mechanics and vehicles, but of course they had their own drivers—expertly trained drivers, I might add.

Air Force Special Operations Command: The Air Force is in the special operations business, too, with their Special Operations forces headquartered at Hurlburt Field in Florida, just inland from Ft. Walton Beach. Commanded by a three-star, three of their units are machine-based and one of them is human-based. The three machine-based units revolve around the distinct capabilities of the incredibly great aircraft and crews of the AC-130 gunships, the MC-130 transports, and the MH-53 helicopters. I say "machine-based" not to downgrade the great people working those machines, but rather to say that their goal is to get the machines to do the work.

The human-based capabilities are parachute medics (called PJ's, parachute jumpers) and STS, special tactics squadron. The STS are small detachments of airmen that can attach into a special ops unit of any type and control close air support (CAS). By that I mean they call in airstrikes. I had several STS airmen assigned to SF A-teams to help them call in air cover. I had Air Force planners at my headquarters who would help plan air missions for jets and bombers, and air support anywhere we needed it across the country.

One of the reasons our Army stood up Special Forces as a branch years ago was so we could grow the expertise needed with professional UW operators, not just temporary UW operators. By the time I took command of the Joint force in Afghanistan, I'd spent years learning the ropes. I'd jumped out of MC-130s, flown in MH-53 helicopters, and worked with PJs and STS for two decades... and that's why you couldn't put a conventional commander in there because he/she hadn't done that for the last twenty years. So I was very comfortable with their capabilities and what they could do. Great medics, great forward air controllers (FACs), and the AC-130 gunships are awesome. Every Green Beret on the planet loves to know that an AC-130 "Specter" gunship is above.

Unlike Green Berets, Rangers or SEALs, the Air Force spec ops airmen normally just call themselves AFSOC (Air Force Special Operations Command), or sometimes you hear the term "Air Commandos," but not often. By its nature, AFSOC is very equipment-based. The Air Force spec ops people execute with their airplanes, a hand-in-glove capability that's different from personal execution of a mission in something like, say, hand-to-hand combat or underwater demolition. The Army is all about soldiers of flesh and blood. Same with the SEALs, and thus the names. The Air Force is aerial precision strikes and mobility. Awesome.

Marine Special Operations: The most recent special operations force is— the Marines. The Marines just recently stood up a special operations capability which is really a combination of a unilateral striker force and some foreign internal defense capabilities.

U.S. Army Special Operations Command: U.S. Army Special Operations Command (USASOC) is headquartered in Ft. Bragg, North Carolina, with a three-star commander. USASOC, the biggest player in USSOCOM, has five elements. There's a Special Forces Command that has seven Special Forces groups, five active and two National Guard. There is also the John F. Kennedy Special Warfare Center, which trains future Special Forces Soldiers. USASOC also has Civil Affairs and Psychological Operations Command (USACAPOC), a two-star command, which has the Army Civil Affairs and the Army Psychological Operations. They're grouped together only by coincidence. PSYOP and CA are different missions, executed by different people. Both of those specialties are mostly in the Army Reserve. Very few are in the regular army. Civil Affairs, as the name implies, really helps societies, villages, and communities enhance some of their civil infrastructure to mitigate some of the overall frustration. USASOC also has the 75th Ranger Regiment and the 160th Special Operations Aviation Regiment.

I had a Civil Affairs company in Afghanistan and they were able to get locals to help build medical clinics, hospitals and other similar efforts. There are civil affairs agricultural teams, economic teams, bank infrastructure teams, and political, how-to-set-up-your-own-Congress teams — skills that aren't readily inherent in the active duty military, but are very important to society.

So in a place like Afghanistan where little infrastructure exists, if we can put in a couple of dozen agricultural advisors, it can take local life a thousand years into the future. Von Clausewitz said that war is a continuation of politics by other means. Nowhere is that truer than in Afghanistan, where politics is chaotic, violent and very decentralized. Just like this war. The CA company in my command did not go through the Special Forces qualification course, with the physical and tactical emphasis; they went through a CA course with its own goals and training objectives. It's more of an academic university course.

PSYOP is the other half of the U.S. Army Civil Affairs and Psychological Command (USACAPOC). The objective is to destroy the enemy's *willingness* to wage war, not its *ability* to wage war. The goal of a PSYOP team is to get between the enemy's ears. I had a PSYOP company in my command in Afghanistan and they helped me change the way the enemy thinks. That, in turn, changes the way the enemy acts. If you've worked with all the moving pieces, you understand that in a lot of the operations, the real objective is to change the way the enemy thinks, not the way he operates. According to Sun T-su, that's ultimately the objective of any war — change the way the enemy thinks, thus winning the war because he no longer has a reason to fight. The goal is often better achieved by persuasion than by the gun.

An advantage of being a historian (at least, an amateur) is being able to look across history to learn those lessons. There are many examples when, unlike Sun Tsu, we've reduced the ability of the enemy to wage war, but we haven't changed the willingness to wage war. For instance, look at Milosevic in Bosnia. He lasted longer against the U.S. and all of NATO than France did against the Germans in 1940. He lasted longer against us than France did against Germany — because of his attitude. He was never convinced not to fight.

America has two additional regiments in our Army Special Operations family of assets. One is the 160th Special Operations Aviation Regiment, SOAR, headquartered in Ft. Campbell, Kentucky. The 160th has three types of helicopters, and the men and equipment to turn them into powerful tools of the trade: CH-47s, called Chinooks; MA-60s, called Blackhawks; and AH-6s, called Little Birds. They are awesome helicopters that are souped up to the maximum extent that technology will allow. The pilots are better trained than any other pilots on the planet. They all go through a serious aviation assessment program. They've all started as master pilots in the regular Army before they even started their first day in the SOAR. They all have thousands of flight hours including night-vision flying. The 160th has no fixed-wing aircraft, only rotary-wing assets: choppers, mean ones. The 160th mission is to act as transport and as a fire support platform for special ops soldiers. They service mostly Rangers, SEALs and commandos. They pride themselves on getting to any objective plus or minus 30 seconds of the target time. So if you need to be at the top of the mountain at midnight, they'll get you there plus or minus 30 seconds, with Little Bird gunships providing fire support as you slide down the rope. Absolute precision, no doubt about it.

Back to the unilateral versus unconventional perspective: the 160th is a unilateral force. They move special ops troopers from point A to point B for precise, surgically violent raids. They flew the SEALs into bin Laden's backyard. The 160th specializes in night operations because that's when you can surprise the enemy. And when you're doing a unilateral American raid, you want to do it when America has the advantage, which is at night, because we can see at night and the enemy usually can't.

When you're fighting *by, with and through* the locals, you've got to do it in the daytime, because that's when the locals can see. Afghan soldiers don't have night-vision devices. When fighting an unconventional war, you don't need super-precise, souped-up, nighttime-only helicopters. We need the ability to move massive numbers of indigenous forces across the valley. Surprisingly, that's why Green Berets like me rarely use the 160th. When the generals ask me about the 160th I put it this way: "Sir, the 160th are awesome and I love them. They have a Ferrari that'll go 0 to 60 in about three seconds. And it's really cool. But I have a bunch of migrants that I've got to get from one side of the tobacco farm to the other, to pick tobacco. I just need a couple of good pickup trucks. I need about 2 Ford F150 pickup trucks. I don't need a Ferrari. I don't even want the Ferrari because it can't make it through the tobacco field." The 160th works predominantly with the Rangers and other unilateral SOF.

The second additional Regiment within U.S. Army Special Operations Command is the 75th Rangers. Clearly, they are the best light infantry on earth. They have three battalions of four companies each. First Battalion (my old unit) is at Hunter Army Air Field in Savannah. The Second Ranger Battalion is at Ft. Lewis, Washington. And the Third Battalion and the Regimental Headquarters are at Ft. Beginning, Georgia, home of the infantry.

The last and largest portion of USASOC is Special Forces command, located at Ft. Bragg, with seven Special Forces Groups stationed at different locations. Each group is focused on a different portion of the world. They are regionally and linguistically trained to support war plans at specific locations.

My personal and professional mantra was *Fortune favors the bold,* so I put it all on the line as a young captain: I applied to transfer from the conventional Army to the Special Forces. To get in, I had to pass the Special Forces Qualification Course (SFQC). I'll never forget what the artillery branch management officer, the captain's assignment officer at the Army's Human Resources Command in Alexandria, Virginia, told me over the phone: "OK, Herd, you can go to the SF qualification course if you want to, but remember, about 75% of the guys flunk out of Green Beret school. So *when* you flunk out, we've got something for you."

That gave me a little added incentive to make it through the qualification course. I did not know what that "something" was, but I knew I would not like it. So I got orders to go to SFQC.

"Green Beret" is kind of a Hollywood name, but it's not an official name. I am a Green Beret, yes, but my records say Special Forces–Green

Beret is slang. It's not a derogatory term. And I identify myself as that. Formally, I'll say I'm a Special Forces officer, but among friends we'll say, "Hey, what are you Green Berets doing this weekend?"

Special ops in general, SF especially so, is much less concerned about formality and arbitrary standards than they are about practicality and valuable standards. The decision authority is a lot lower than conventional forces and it has to be that way to succeed at our UW mission.

When I was last deployed, I let my guys grow beards because Afghan men have beards. If you don't have a beard, you're not a man. It's that simple. I didn't ask anybody's permission. I just did it. My men didn't really ask my permission. They just did it because it needed to be done — which is okay, because that is the right answer. They're authorized, in fact required to make tactical decisions. That is why they are so special, and why the majority don't pass the qualification course. SF soldiers need to make decisions based on general intent only.

Take "PT," for example: physical training. Special Forces soldiers train and work out like professional athletes, actually more than many professional athletes. Our whole culture is built around mental and physical toughness. Yet I can count on one hand the times I've done *organized* PT in a large formation. Decentralization is the key to everything in a UW environment. If we can't trust SF soldiers to work out on their own, how can we trust them to do the right thing when they are with 500 tribesmen and some warlord deep in the Hindu Kush?

I worked out almost every day while on each of many deployments, and even today, after having retired, I work out on a regular basis. Old habits. While deployed, I ran a little bit, but mostly I cross-trained on machines. I lifted weights in our gym.

If you put more than 5 SF troopers in an area for more than a month, somehow they'll find or build a gym. Our gym at the HQ was pretty nice, full of weights and machines. It was open 24/7, so I could walk in for a quick set of chin-ups or bench presses between mission briefs, or after my daily battle update.

In Afghanistan, I'd run a couple of times a week around the airfield, which was about a 6- or 8-mile run. The second or third time I ran that route I got almost all of the way around only to find out that they closed the road to clear it for land mines, so I had to run all the way back around. That turned into about a 14- or 15-mile run. I said, "All right, I'm going to plan that one a little better next time." One of the few bad things about being an old paratrooper is that the hips and knees are not kind to running anymore. But few of us will complain, because we know the risks early on and because we've been honored to work with the best.

The only time I did not have a weapon on my body while I was in Afghanistan was when I was in the shower or doing PT. When I was sleeping I had it right next to me. When I took a shower I'd check my weapon into the operations center, called the Joint Operations Center, or JOC. The JOC is a big room with computer screens and maps all around. I would drop my weapon off with the JOC battle captain, the guy running the JOC on a minute-to-minute basis. The JOC was manned by intel folks, operations folks, logisticians and my aviation planners. The battle captain oversees it 24/7. Anytime I wanted to know what was going on, all the answers were right there. We had secure satellite radios to the whole world.

In addition to our own gym, we had our own mess hall. We ate better than anyone else in Afghanistan ... anyone. Every Sunday afternoon, we had a volleyball game and cookout. I let the soldiers out of uniform on Sundays. We played music over the PSYOP loudspeakers. Other than the missing kegs of Budweiser (which were not allowed), we were set for our Sunday picnics. The rest of the units and their headquarters at Bagram were begging to get an invitation to visit us. Somehow the nurses at the Bagram hospital always seemed to get an invitation to our Sunday afternoon garden parties. It was like having your own derby box back at my home in Kentucky. Everybody wants to be your friend. All this happens because you've got good people and you want to make it as pleasant as possible.

10

Earning the Green Beret

Years before I could even imagine commanding the Special Operations Task Force in Afghanistan, I began the six-month Special Forces qualification course at Ft. Bragg, North Carolina, in January of 1989. I enjoyed it, did fairly well, and passed it, because, again, my entire life had focused on athletic team sports, navigating through the woods, and having a good time with good soldiers.

The first phase of that course was a 30-day training and testing period. Really, that part was an assessment period where we did a lot of weeding out of soldiers. I think we lost 75 percent of our class during that phase. Some got hurt, some flunked out, and some just couldn't take the stress and quit. Literally every couple of hours, we'd look out the window or through the pine trees and see a former fellow student dragging his gear out of the billets and into the waiting truck to take him from Camp McCall on the outskirts of Ft. Bragg, back to the main post. We called that the "duffle bag drag." The first month or so was mostly physical training, small unit tactics, land navigation, patrolling through the woods, and duffle bag drags.

During the early portion of the SFQC, we lived in small team hootches at McCall. "Hootch" is military slang for a hut or lean-to. Given a couple of good field soldiers and enough time, a poncho lean-to "hootch" will get transformed into a mansion. The hootches near Ft Bragg never made that transformation. They were old cabins with tar paper over the outside. They slept one 12-man A-team. At any given time during the night, we had to have one man awake and alert as a fire watch.

We produced a simple fire watch schedule (fire watch is an old-school term for watching out for a fire, but we use it today to mean

38

guarding your buddies). Every man was on duty for one hour. After that, he'd wake up the next man on the list. We started the list at one end of the room and simply went down the row of bunks one man at a time. Every one of the 12 men in the hootch was on duty every other night.

One of the great mysteries in my hootch was why we used one extra man each night. Why did it take seven men to pull six one-hour tours of duty, or why did five men pull hour-long shifts when we only got four hours of sleep? After a couple of nights of this mystery, we began to reconstruct the scene of the crime. Smith in bunk number one was on duty from 2200 hours to 2300 hours, then he woke up Jones in bunk number two for duty from 2300 to 2400 hours, and so on. Yet, when it was time for the two foreign officers in my team to pull their duty, we discovered that they were only pulling duty for five or ten minutes, just long enough for the man that they relieved to go back to sleep. As soon as he was asleep, they'd wake up their replacement, which of course was some 50 or 55 minutes early. We eventually found them out and confronted them only to hear our classmate from southern Africa say, "In my country we have enlisted soldiers to pull guard duty."

We worked with several of the foreign officers in SFQC. America uses training slots in various American military schools as part of a military engagement program. The thinking is that if we invite several junior officers of developing countries to attend American military schools, when they become national leaders they will have positive feelings toward America and our culture. The SFQC was the first time I worked with foreign officers on a regular basis.

A couple of weeks into the first phase of the training, we had our final night land navigation test. This was a high-pressure event where each SF candidate had to navigate some 15 kilometers at night carrying his combat gear and find about five points spread out in the woods, swamps and fields. There were very strict rules about working alone, talking to no one, and not using any lights. Halfway through the course, I almost tripped over one of our allied officers from the Middle East. He was lost and leaning up against a tree at about 0100 hours. "Excuse me," he said as he walked over to me holding his map and a flashlight. "Where am I?"

I immediately found myself in a dilemma. Do I break the rules about talking and using a light and tell him where he is and risk failing the course? Or do I help this poor Arab, who's never seen so many trees in his whole life? Even as a young Green Beret candidate, I knew that working *by, with and through* others was the key to success. "We're right here, by this trail intersection," I said as I pointed to the map.

I pointed to a hill on the horizon and said: "North is that way."

Then I double-timed it along my previous azimuth to escape the crime scene just in case it was a setup.

At the end of that first month phase of the SFQC, I found myself in a patrol base just a couple of days before we were scheduled to come home to end that 30-day "phase one." Early one morning my instructor's radio rang out. "Instructor bravo two seven, this is the exercise control base. Have Captain Herd bring all of his gear and report to the cadre in a truck at the following grid coordinates...."

I looked at my instructor and asked him what was up and he said, "I don't know. Get your stuff and come with me."

I was the captain on our team which meant that I was the A-team commander in our course, so I went to my assistant A-team leader, a great sergeant from one of the three Ranger battalions, and said: "Hey, I don't know what's going on. But I'm taking my kit so I guess I'm not coming back. You're in charge. Good luck. Move out when you are ready."

We went down to the intersection at the appropriate grid coordinate and linked up with the cadre as directed. They said, "Herd, your wife is okay, but your house just burned down. We're going to take you back to Fayetteville. Don't worry. You passed the first phase. You did a great job. We'll take you back, link you up with your wife, and you can link up with the rest of the class on Monday."

My wife Ann and I had begun dating when we were juniors in high school. I tell people I started dating my wife when she was only 16, but that since we're from Kentucky it's no big deal. In fact, I was only 17 myself, so it really wasn't a big deal. We dated the last part of high school. We dated through college. We dated when she was in graduate school at the University of Tennessee and I was a lieutenant at Ft. Stewart and Hunter. We married just a couple of years before the SF qualifications course. But this was the first time we had been able to live together because Ann had been at the University of Tennessee graduate school and had just gotten her doctorate when we moved to Ft. Bragg for the SF qualifications course. So when I got that call, we'd lived in the same house for literally only one night of our marriage. Lo and behold, the house burned down while I was gone. Thank goodness Ann was not hurt. The noise and the smoke woke her up in the middle of the night. She broke some glass and was able to crawl out a window. By the time the fire department got there, the house was partially burned down, but thank God my high school sweetheart was okay.

So they took me out of the field and I met Ann back at Ft. Bragg. We gave each other a big hug, then went back and surveyed the house. It wasn't completely burned to the ground but it was certainly damaged. A lot of our household goods were ruined. Much of our wedding china and crystal was damaged. But again, thank God she was okay. And thank God I had passed that first phase and that I would be able to link up with my buddies in two days! I did not want to do that phase again, or return to "something special" that the Artillery was saving for me.

When my wife picked me up at the company area, I'd been gone for a month. I was dirty and tired and hungry and cold because it was February. One of the things I did right away was take my boots off for the first time in a couple of weeks. For several days I had known my feet were sore, but I assumed it was because I had been walking all day for most of the last month. But when I took my boots off, my left foot ballooned up, doubling in size.

My wife had cut her hand while breaking the glass to crawl out of the window and she had to get some stitches, so we went to the SF aid station there at Ft. Bragg. I said, "Hey, Doc, while I'm here, take a look at my foot. It's killing me and it's about twice the size that it's supposed to be."

Well, he looked at it and said, "Hey, stud, you've got cellulitis. Your foot and halfway up to your left knee is infected. You need surgery and you're going to the hospital immediately."

I said, "Doc, I can't go to the hospital immediately. I'm going to link up with my class again on Monday, just day after tomorrow. I just finished phase one, I've got to continue on in the Special Forces qualification course."

He said, "Pal, if you don't get to the hospital now we're going to cut your foot and leg off because gangrene is starting to set in."

So they sliced open my foot and I spent the next week in the hospital. I had been in the field for a month, my house burned down, and then I went straight to the hospital for a week. But it was all a blessing. Had I not been pulled from the field a few days early, I'm certain I would have persevered to finish and the gangrene could have spread. I may very well have lost my left foot and leg, and possibly my life.

After the surgery, I was in the hospital recovering. That night the nurse came in with a little list and said, "Okay, check off what you want for breakfast tomorrow morning and we'll bring it in for you."

I said, "Well, okay. How many items can I check?"

She said, "I don't know. Check whatever you want, I guess." Now, remember, I'd been in the field for a month. I was pretty hungry. So I checked everything they had. Every morning for the next week I had eggs, bacon, sausage, pancakes, waffles, orange juice and coffee for breakfast. I was living the dream and with all the blankets I could use. One of my SF buddies even brought me a cold beer. Probably against the hospital rules, but who wants to be subject to such silly rules?

But I did eventually get well and I did link up with my SF classmates. I missed about two weeks of training in the middle of the qualifications course, but I made it up at the end of the course. No problem.

11

Special Forces History and the "Coin"

The Special Forces Regiment traces its legacy back to World War II and the creation of the OSS, the Office of Strategic Services. The OSS began under Wild Bill Donovan during World War II. Donovan earned the Medal of Honor during World War I, and later was key in starting the CIA after World War II. Among other things, the OSS parachuted small detachments called "Jedburg" teams in to Nazi-occupied France to organize the Resistance and support the unconventional war aspects of the European Theater of War. The father of Special Forces, Col. Aaron Bank, whom I have met, died at the age of 101 while I was in Afghanistan. He jumped into France as a young captain, a Jedburg detachment commander. After the war, he founded the original Special Forces Group, which was 10th Group, my regiment, in 1951 as a lieutenant colonel. Just as now, their task was to conduct unconventional warfare in Europe.

So think about the 1950s. We built 10th Group out of a cadre of old OSS troopers from World War II, other soldiers, paratroopers, Rangers from the war, and a huge number of displaced Europeans who had joined the U.S. Army under the Lodge Act. That law, named after Henry Cabot Lodge, allowed foreigners to gain U.S. citizenship after a successful tour in the military. So if you were a Pole, a Ukrainian or an East German who could not go home because the Soviets now ran your nation and who wanted to be an American, you could get citizenship after serving in our Army.

When those future American citizens joined our Army, we were looking for people who spoke Central European languages and had a familiarity with military operations, particularly in Central Europe — a perfect match because our army at this time had lots of Poles and Ukrainians and East Germans. Many of them joined Special Forces. They went through Special Forces selection and training and then joined 10th Group, which was chartered to conduct unconventional warfare in Europe.

Among the great traditions of our Army, 10th Special Forces Group is where the unusual tradition of the military challenge coin began. Since we had so many Central Europeans in the 10th Group back in the 1950s with so many languages and so many backgrounds, to identify each other when we met covertly we used a coin, a medallion, as a bona fide. If I put my coin on the table and you put yours on the table then we were the same regiment. If I put mine on the table and you didn't have one, then you were probably a Soviet spy and you had to be killed. From this a tradition was born, and today every unit has a coin.

Now the tradition is: if I put my coin on the table and you don't, then you have to buy me a beer. But if you put yours on the table and I don't have mine, then I have to buy you a beer. Much kinder and gentler that it used to be! I've had a coin on my body almost 24/7 since I was a lieutenant. I carry my SF coin in my wallet and my Ranger coin on my keychain. I just realized at one point that I have over a hundred coins.

That coin tradition has now spread throughout the U.S. government and throughout the world militaries. When I commanded 3rd Battalion of 10th Special Forces Group, we designed and minted our own coin with crossed skis, superimposed over a snowflake with a large military rucksack in the center. On the other side, we put master parachutist wings and our regimental motto, "de Oppresso Liber" — to liberate the oppressed. When I commanded 3rd Special Forces Group forward deployed in Afghanistan, we designed a coin with master parachutist wings superimposed over crossed arrows (the insignia of a Special Forces soldier), all superimposed over a map of Afghanistan. Under that we had the words "by, with and through" printed. I gave that coin to great soldiers, sailors, marines and airmen as a small sign of my appreciation for their service.

Now, a lot of myth clouds one highly publicized part of our Green Beret legacy. Here are the facts. In 1961 President John F. Kennedy came for a tour of Ft. Bragg. He wanted to see this relatively new and unheard-of unconventional warfare capability that America had.

The SF headgear had been a beret, not a helmet, because of the Central European legacy of our organization. For example, French soldiers typically wore berets. So when they came into our Army and we created our own unconventional Central European organization, the beret was the headgear of choice. But big regular Army had outlawed the Green Beret. It was not in accordance with Army regulation and the SF troopers of the 1950s were not allowed to wear it without risk.

Being good soldiers, all of the Green Berets at Ft. Bragg followed that regulation ... except when President Kennedy came for a visit. Right before his plane landed they donned the Green Beret. At the end of the visit he proclaimed, "You're authorized to wear that Green Beret as a mark of courage and a badge of distinction." On that tour of Ft. Bragg he awarded the Green Beret to the earliest Special Forces soldiers "as a mark of courage and a badge of distinction." And that's why we wear the Green Beret today.

12

Special Forces Training

By a stroke of luck, after I finished the SF Qualification Course, I was able to attend the Military Freefall (MFF) course at Ft. Bragg. Between my time in the Ranger battalion and the SFQC, I probably jumped 50 times or so using a static line parachute. With those chutes, you walk to the jump door with one hand on your reserve parachute and the other holding the static line close to the jumper cable attached to the airplane. When you jump, you exit the airplane feet first, slight bend at the waist, with your hands over the ripcord for the reserve. The plane usually slows down a little so you don't get the stuffing knocked out of you, but that's it. The line attached to your main chute is 20 feet long. At precisely 20 feet and about one inch, your chute is opening and you are floating to earth. That's static line parachute jumping.

The MFF School taught paratroopers how to jump using a different type of parachute. There we learned to use parachutes without static lines. I remember my first jump with a freefall parachute rig. I knew that I was going to hit 120 miles per hour in the freefall — terminal velocity for a jumper — so anything that the wind could work on, anything like a tab of a collar that was loose, would beat me up pretty good. So, nothing is loose, we always jump in an aerodynamic jumpsuit. At the higher altitudes, above about 17,000 feet, we use oxygen. At those altitudes we have an oxygen mask on our faces and a small bottle of oxygen that we're going to need to use until we get down to denser air. You can freefall for two or three minutes and open your chute at a low altitude called High Altitude Low Opening, or HALO, or jump and open it pretty quickly at a high altitude and drift down in near silence from HAHO, or High Altitude High Opening.

A very small number, just a couple of hundred special operators, become MFF qualified every year. The bulk of those are Special Forces with a few Rangers as well. The Army Military Freefall School has a partnership with the Air Force so that the USAF provides the airplanes and we give them a certain number of student slots in every class. So there are a few Air Force parajumpers, PJs, who are part of the AF Special Operations Command, which is a part of USSOCOM, who go through every year, and perhaps a few SEALs every year as well. So approximately a couple of hundred soldiers, sailors, and airmen a year earn their MFF wings. When I went through the course, it was mostly at Ft. Bragg. They have since moved it to Yuma, Arizona, because the air and atmosphere and wind conditions are more favorable there. There is never any wind. There are never any clouds. Just good, clear skies every day.

Years later, as a battalion commander, I frequently got requests from the men to go to HALO school, but very seldom got a request from someone to attend the much tougher combat diving program (SCUBA), the Special Forces Underwater Operations Course. There are two types of divers: working divers and combat divers. Working divers do underwater salvage; they fix things such as bridges. They are also called hardhat divers. The Navy runs the underwater working-diver school.

And then there are combat divers, which consist of SEAL and SF troopers, plus a few in the Marines—the Fleet Marine Force for beach reconnaissance and that sort of thing; a few in the Air Force in their PJ Force; and a few Rangers in their recon units. But that's about it. The bulk of the combat divers are SEALs or SF troopers.

As a captain, I commanded a combat diver, or sometimes called a *scuba* detachment. When I finished the qualification course I applied for one of the possible follow-on courses, because I was already at Bragg and thought I would get another school while I was there. I applied for the combat diver course because I grew up swimming. And they said, "Did you swim in college?" I said, "No, I didn't swim in college but I'm a pretty good swimmer." They said, "Well, you're already a jumpmaster, so why don't you go to HALO school instead?" So I said, "Sure. I'll go to HALO school." And I did.

But when I got to 10th Group and walked in the door and reported, they said, "Hey, you're a HALO guy. That's great. I don't need a HALO captain, but we're building a combat diver team. What do you think about that?" And I said, "Perfect! Sign me up." So I got lucky. And I would literally become one of a very small handful of people in Special Forces who was both HALO and Scuba certified. When I retired, there were about a dozen Special Forces colonels in the Army that were dual certified, HALO and Combat Diver. A dozen max.

The free-fall parachuting has always fascinated my civilian friends, so let me tell you a little about it. If you make a mistake when jumping out of a plane, you're just as dead from two thousand feet as you are from twenty thousand feet, it's all the same. But, really, you're safer at a higher altitude because you have more time to fix any mistakes. So HALO, High Altitude Low Opening, is jumping from an extremely high altitude and opening your parachute at a low altitude. The Low Opening part is usually at about four thousand feet above the earth. Regardless of where you jump, you open at four thousand feet. The higher you jump, the more time you have to get flat and stable before you have to pull the rip cord. The first several jumps we did were at about 12,000 or 13,000 feet. When you fall, you fall ten seconds per 1,000 feet. So if you do the math that's maybe a minute and a half to get stable from when you jump at, say, 12,000 feet and when you pull at 4,000 feet. And being stable is very important. A lot of people will jump and immediately spin or tumble when they jump because their body position is off. For whatever reason, I never spun and I never tumbled. You reach terminal velocity, which is 120 miles an hour, in the first five seconds or so.

Here are the basic differences. When free-fall jumping you pull your own chute. It's strapped on like a backpack. You've got a harness over your shoulder, a harness around the top of your legs and then a belly strap. You've got the reserve on the bottom back and the main on the top of the back with two ripcords, one for each chute. You have the primary ripcord on the right hand. You pull that and the main opens. In the left hand is your reserve. When you pull that, it cuts away the main and deploys the reserve. You don't want two chutes. These are square chutes with a lot of forward momentum and if there are two of them inflated above you, they can go towards each other and deflate each other.

They both have a forward movement of about eighteen knots. So if you have one, you're going forward at eighteen knots. But if two of them are up and they happen to be turned towards each other, they could both collapse, giving no lift whatsoever. This actually is very possible if you have a malfunction that drives you to pull your reserve anyway. If something goes wrong, it means you were spinning, or got your legs through the parachute's riser, or the main didn't fully deploy or partially deployed, etc. They are a flying wing. That's how they're basically designed. So pulling the reserve automatically cuts away the main on our military free-fall rigs.

With HALO you've got your main parachute on your back and then you've got your rucksack full of your combat gear which is snapped on in front of you above your knees, lying on top of your knees. And you've got that cinched up real tight to your belly band and then real tight around your legs with your weapon strapped down on one side of your rucksack. All of that has to be real tight because everything reacts with the flow of air, and at 120 miles per hour the smallest piece of fabric can turn into a wing and start you spinning or worse.

If anything is off-center a little bit, the whole body spins. So you must correct that immediately. If it's a little cockeyed to the left, you'll have to put your right arm out a little further or bend your left leg back a little further to counteract the rucksack tilt. And you've got to figure out all of these solutions as you're flying 120 miles an hour through the darkness toward the hard ground.

You need oxygen when you jump above 12,500 feet. If you're above that, you take an oxygen mask out of the door with you. You've got that on you as you jump — a small oxygen tank about the size of a tennis ball container, of course with a tube going to your face mask that covers your mouth and nose. If you're flying at 12,000 feet but the plane quickly flies up to 13 or 14 to jump, then you'd be okay without oxygen. We did, in fact, start our first jumps below oxygen with no equipment and then graduate up to nighttime combat equipment with oxygen, from 20,000 feet or so. The oxygen mask is just one more complicating factor, one more thing to get crooked and cause stability problems.

At HALO you can jump out at about 160—180 knots. Static line jumps are much slower — about 110 knots depending on the type of air-craft. In bigger airplanes you can go a little bit faster. Bigger airplanes sometimes can't slow down much more than that. I've done both static line and free-fall out of C-130s, C-17s, C-5s, MC-130s, UH-60s, CH 47s, UH-1s, even an old Russian MI-8 (HIP), and probably a few I don't remember!

There are two ways to exit a military aircraft with free-fall gear. You can stand on the tailgate and then turn around in the air and face the airplane so that you look at the airplane as it flies away. That way, by design, your head is up and your belly is down, which helps you keep flat and stable. Or you can dive out doing a belly flop or a racing dive. As soon as you leave the aircraft you arch your back so that your belt buckle is the lowest part of your body. You want your center of gravity to be your belt buckle.

With MFF you can do the same kinds of exits from the side door as you do from the tailgate, but the side doors are more complicated because you have the wind hitting your side it can often cause a spin.

The release point at altitude depends on the wind, which the jump-masters take into consideration when planning the jump. The drop zone's location as well as the direction and speed of the wind, along with the plane's altitude and speed, will all be part of the jumpmaster's consideration on where the ideal release point is.

There's another technique called HAHO — high altitude, high opening — in which you jump high and immediately pull and then you can fly maybe 20, 30, 40 miles from exiting the plane to the drop zone. You've got to really work on the wind speed and direction and it's an aeronautical navigation exercise at that point. From the perspective of the guy on the ground, you don't hear the jumpers coming in. You can hear a brief flutter of the nylon about twenty feet up and that's about it. That, or the snap of a bullet.

As soon as you get flat and stable, you do two or three things. You get situational awareness—what's going on around you. Do you have any fellow jumpers that are in your way? Two: Are you, in fact, flat and stable, or perhaps slowly spinning? Three: You've got to identify the right direction so you can track where you're going — the drop zone. It is a challenge to fly 120 miles per hour through space and still look for the right drop zone so you can face it and know where you're going. What I always did was immediately gain altitude awareness by looking at my altimeter, like a large wristwatch that I wore on my left wrist, maybe two inches in diameter with glow-in-the-dark numbers on it, that I would set while still on the ground and then would double-check when I was at altitude.

The jumpmaster would give you an altitude prior to the jump — Okay, we're at 10,000 feet" — and you check and make sure it says that. There's a fair amount of science involved in the process. And the jumpmaster does that math as well, to make sure you're tracking. At night you put a small chem-light on the altimeter. That is a small plastic vial about the size of a cigar, filled with a glow-in-the-dark liquid. The Army runs on chem-lights. You tape most of it up so that there's just a little bit of it shining through. You tape it onto the side so you can see the arm of the altimeter go around.

As soon as you get out, you maintain stability, get and maintain situational awareness, and look at your altimeter. You don't want to freeze on your altimeter because you can kind of lock onto it and then just forget everything else: bad mistake! So I would just look now and again, just like driving a car — look ahead, left, right — practice moving my hands so I can find my ripcord so that I don't panic at the last minute. I make sure I know right where it is. Even if it's right where it's supposed to be, if your harness is a little loose or the wind may have moved it a little off-center and it's on your shoulder as opposed to on your chest, it's only three or four inches but it's a really important three or four inches when you're looking for it!

So you continue to look at your altimeter, gauge your rate of descent, make sure you're tracking okay every 500 feet. Thinking, "I know where I am. I know what I'm doing. I'm starting to get pretty close so I have another two or three looks and I'll be ready to pull." And then when you pull, you can't just bring your right arm in because that will turn you into a spin. You have to simultaneously put your left arm out because it's all aerodynamics, just like wings of an airplane, as you bring your right arm in to the ripcord. So you practice that prior to pull.

Then when you get it, you pull vigorously all the way out, looking at your hand to make sure you've got the ripcord all the way out. And then within a half a second, you find yourself going twenty miles an hour instead of 120 miles an hour. I can remember 100 times seeing the parachute through my boots as the chute engaged and flipped me upside down. My feet are all the way over me as I'm upside down for just a brief second, and then they swing back down to the bottom, of course.

In the mission preparation and the jumpmaster briefing, you ID all the jump zones on maps. You identify key terrain features. Maybe a river, maybe a big city to the east, maybe a blinking water tower or something like that. So you find a known point, then in your mind you say, "From that point, the river, or the water tower, or the bridge, or the football stadium — something with lights — I know it's north roughly 500 meters." You need to make sure you know where the release point is in relationship to the known point. In your mind you're saying, "All right, I want to follow the aircraft because the release point is before the drop zone." So the airplane drops you and then flies over the drop zone. So in your eyes you're following the aircraft and the drop zone's ahead of you. Or maybe you're going the other way, depending on wind. So it could be you don't follow the aircraft. You go away from the aircraft and that means you're going toward the drop zone.

Your release point could be left or right, fore or aft of the DZ, depending on the wind. The plane will normally drop you upwind of the drop zone. So as soon as you pull the ripcord, the first point of performance is to check for canopy and gain canopy control. It's natural that you look up and see you've got a canopy, all the risers are attached, there're no holes bigger than your head. Little holes — "okay." Big holes — "cut away."

Big holes rip and they get bigger. So if you see any, cut away and start with the other chute. Then you reach up with both hands and grab the two toggle switches, which are sticks about half as long as a cigar. They are Velcroed into the risers. The risers are coming from your shoulders. About a foot above your shoulders, they split — two to the front, two to the rear. Sewn on to the rear panel is a little pocket for the toggle switch.

The toggle switches are attached with cords to the flaps at the back of the parachute. When you pull the sticks down, that's closing the back flaps on the back of the chute. Pull them both down and your forward thrust slows. Pull just one down, one side slows, the other side speeds up so you turn left or right. When you pull them both down about eye-level, you're at about half brakes and you travel forward at about half speed. At no brakes, they rest well above your head and you fly forward more quickly. Pull them all the way down to your knees and you're at full brakes. What every jumper does as soon as he or she is under canopy is to kind of test them out. Turn to the left. Turn to the right. Make sure your ability to steer works. If you want to gain SA, situational awareness, do a 360-degree circle just to see what's around you. Make sure there are no jumpers coming your way.

The lower jumper always has the right of way. You can't tell what's above you because there's a parachute up there and it blocks your vision. So you can't see if there's someone above you. But you can see if there's someone below you. So the lower jumper always has the right of way. If somebody below you is coming from your right to left, then you steer away from him because he probably can't see you. As you approach the drop zone, you want to make sure you're going into the wind. You can do that a couple of ways.

If it's daytime, or sometimes at night, you can look at the wind in the trees or flags, smoke or water caps—face the wind. And if all else fails, my personal favorite is to spit into the wind and see which way it goes. I spit and it comes back or goes to the left or right; just follow that. So, check canopy, gain canopy control, look out for fellow jumpers, prepare to land so that as you go in you're facing the wind. You're at the right altitude and you find the right drop zone. The advantage of free-fall jumpers is that square parachutes are much more steerable and therefore they can land on much smaller drop zones.

When I came back from Afghanistan, my next command was of the Army's marketing brigade that supports recruiting for officers and enlisted. That brigade consists of three battalions. One is the Army Marksmanship Team at Ft. Benning, filled with Olympic and world-class shooters. Another battalion, located at Ft. Knox, Kentucky, is filled with souped-up Hummers and tractor trailers that travel the country telling the Army story to potential soldiers. The third battalion in that brigade is the Army Parachute Team, the "Golden Knights." They are an awesome group of soldiers and paratroopers that allows the American people to meet some of their soldiers up close and see some of the terrific capabilities our Army has. I made my last parachute jump with them. A good way to end it. The Golden Knights or an SF

HALO team could land in my parents' front yard. A static line team could probably land somewhere in a football field, but an MFF jumper could land specifically on the 50-yard line. Something the Golden Knights did on a regular basis was jump the football into college bowl games for the Army's PR efforts. A round chute is like a pickup truck, a square MFF chute is like a Ferrari.

The biggest problem with a free-fall jump is not getting stable. If you pull the ripcord while you are spinning out of control, you risk tangling your chute and getting it wrapped around your body because you're tumbling — you could get your legs through the risers or somehow messed up — and then you can't use your reserve chute because it's all tied up too.

A friend of mine couldn't get stable and blacked out when he went through training. He was spinning so hard, the blood went into the brain and he had two massive black eyes and blacked out. Luckily, the parachute has an RRD, ripcord release device, which is a safety mechanism set to an altimeter at 2500 feet. So if all else fails, even if you're dead, at 2500 feet the thing's going to release. That's really the only safety mechanism built in. It saved my friend's life, but he never jumped free-fall again.

The RRD kicked off and my friend floated to the ground like a bag of rocks. He was escorted to the hospital and then home. He didn't graduate. He flunked out. There's a pretty high attrition rate, not because it's physically that hard. The psychology of jumping out of an airplane is significant at that altitude, and then the aerodynamics of maintaining stability are challenging as well. If you're unstable maybe two or three jumps, you're deemed a safety hazard and not allowed to continue. It's not uncommon to see a lot of guys flunk out of MFF training.

Another good buddy of mine broke both his tibia and fibula on a free-fall jump while landing with the wind. He got a compound fracture with the bones sticking out of his leg. He landed with the wind to his back and his leading leg was straight but he just came down too hard. When he landed, he was probably going forward 30 miles an hour. That is why one of my rules was "when all else fails, fall down and roll with it." The other is "always face the wind."

So when I walked back to the jump door for my first MFF jump, I had one hand on the wall of the plane, partially out of habit and partially trying to stabilize myself. The instructor looked deep into my eyes and yelled over the engines, "What are you holding on for, you're going to jump?"

At that point I looked out of the jump door, 12,500 feet to the drop zone at Ft. Bragg, and realized I was at least partially crazy. Three weeks and about 20 free-fall jumps later, my jump buddy and I jumped into the darkness, with rucksacks and rifles strapped to our legs, and oxygen masks over our faces as we made our graduation jump from the MFF course. I think my highest MFF jump was from 22,000 feet and my lowest MFF parachute opening was around 3,500 feet. My static line jumps ranged from about 500 feet to 1,500 feet high.

13

Reporting to the Regiment

After the Military Free Fall course I reported to 3rd Battalion, Tenth Special Forces Group at Ft. Devens, Massachusetts, as a brand-new Green Beret. I was happy to be there. I took command of a Special Forces A-team. An A-team, also called Special Forces Operational Detachment Alpha, is the backbone of Special Forces. "A" teams consist of twelve men. A captain is the detachment commander, and he has a warrant officer as his executive officer. There is an operations sergeant who is similar to an infantry company's first sergeant. He is the noncommissioned officer in charge of that detachment. That person has an assistant who is an E7 / sergeant first class, and is the intelligence officer. There are two communications sergeants with the most up-to-date, long-range, secure communications gear on the planet. There are two engineers or demolition sergeants who give the team the capability to conduct demolition operations, and two weapons sergeants who are experts in all kinds of weapons and small unit tactics. Finally, the team has two medical sergeants who can perform minor surgery almost as well as doctors. All of these men are either noncommissioned officers or warrant officers with an officer as a commander.

All of these men were in the top 25 percent of their respective classes that graduated from the SF Qualification Course at Ft. Bragg. They were all the best of the best. My team, Operational Detachment Alpha zero nine two (ODA 092), was blessed with some great sergeants, many of whom had experience in the Ranger regiment as I did, and all of whom had a lot of Special Forces experience.

ODAs or, as we more commonly called them, "A-teams," are given numbers, not letters, to identify them. My conventional Army captain counterparts command "company A" or "company B." But Special Forces captains command ODAs or A-teams with a detachment number. My team was 092, and it broke out like this. The zero indicated we were in 10th Group, one zero. Tenth Group is the original Special Forces group founded by Col. Banks in 1951 to conduct unconventional warfare in Europe. From here we trace the growth of Special Forces in general. Nine indicated the 9th company in tenth group, also called Charlie Company, 3rd Battalion. Two was the number of the detachment. Each company has six detachments. I was in ODA 092, 10th Group, Charlie Company 3rd Battalion, 2nd detachment.

When I got to that detachment I got to know the soldiers. Man, was I happy to be there! We immediately began to do garrison and field exercises together. Each detachment member would cross-train the rest of us on his specialty. The medics, for instance, would train us on giving IV's and how to stop various types of bleeding. I expect I'm one of the very few folks around that has given himself stitches. We all had to put stitches in our own arms one day for our medical training. All in a day's work.

One day, I went to a meeting at company headquarters with my company commander, a major, and all the other detachment commanders (all captains). We received news that each of the Army's five active-duty Special Forces Groups were reorganizing so that each company would have a military free-fall detachment along with an underwater infiltration or scuba detachment.

That way, each SF company had the ability to get unconventional warfare soldiers (Green Berets) into the enemy-controlled area by HALO, scuba, or overland. What that meant was that an "A" team could infiltrate into an enemy's area by High Altitude, Low Opening parachute (HALO, which is one option under MFF, which I described earlier); by waterborne or underwater infiltration; or, of course, over land, via static line parachute or from a helicopter. Basically, this meant that we could parachute into *any* drop zone — land or water — and run our mission.

So the five other detachment commanders and I, along with the company commander, sat in a meeting to determine how we would break down this requirement (or *opportunity*, as I saw it). Now even though I was HALO/MFF qualified, we had to qualify as an ODA for the mission, and that meant taking another demanding course. Having grown up as a swimmer and having enjoyed the water my whole life, I immediately volunteered my ODA for the Special Forces scuba mission, which meant we would all go to the very challenging Special Forces Under Water Operation Course (SFUWO) at our scuba school in Key West, Florida.

After I left the company headquarters, I went back to the detachment meeting room. I said, "Guys, gather around. I've got some great news for you."

Everybody came around their desks, pulled up a chair and someone said, "Sir, what is it? What's going on? What did y'all talk about at the meeting?"

"092's being redesignated a scuba team," I said. "We're all going to get to go to pre-scuba training and then scuba school in Key West, Florida. Then we're going to have the mission to infiltrate the enemy's area via underwater or on the surface of the sea."

Well, that was very exciting for me ... and for about half of my team. A couple of my team members looked at me in disbelief and said with their eyes, "Sir, I can't *believe* you volunteered us for that. What the heck are you thinking?"

Scuba school is probably the most physically demanding school the Army has. It is thirty days of utterly punishing physical exercise combined with an unforgiving water environment. To give you an idea, in our class of about 50 young men, all Special Forces, Rangers and a few marines, we began the course with a physical fitness test of pushups, sit-ups and a two mile run. I ran the two-miles in 11:05, my fastest time before or since. I was about in the middle of the pack; about 20 or 25 guys ran faster than I did that day even though I set a personal record. Tough.

We all went through a pre-scuba training course before we went to Florida, and I trained myself to swim 75 meters underwater without coming up for air. That's three lengths of a 25-meter pool with no breaths after the start.

I was still physically smoked (worn-out) from the very beginning of the course, but I did it. The first week of the school is called *pool week*. You practice recovering from a series of drowning exercises in the controlled environment of the pool. Really the objective is to get your water confidence up to a point where no matter what happens to you above or below the surface of the water — with scuba tanks and combat gear strapped on your body — you have the presence of mind to calmly and rationally fix the problem with the few seconds of air you have left in your lungs.

The hardest exercise of that week for me was something called "bobbing." In that exercise, we donned twin 80s (two 80 cubic feet high-pressure scuba tanks), about a 10-pound weight belt, BC (buoyancy compensator), fins and mask. All added up, that was about 100 pounds of gear. Of note is that we had no regulator (and thus no air), our fins were on our hands, not our feet, and our BC was empty (and thus provided no lift, only drag). For this drill, we had to go to the deep end of the pool and "bob" for two minutes. You certainly can't tread water for two minutes with all that weight, so the key is to rest on the bottom of the pool. Every few seconds, you push off the bottom with your legs for all you are worth and break the surface of the water long enough to catch a lungful of air. The timing is everything. With a perfect push, you can get your face out of the water about 2 inches. Your lips will remain out of the water for perhaps half of a second until gravity overwhelms your strength and the lead tanks take you back to the bottom. After the first lungful of water, I learned to exhale on the way up and to minimize my wasted efforts on the top.

The second week we learned open-circuit operations and navigation with open-circuit tanks, scuba tanks, typically twin 80s on our backs, cylinders that hold 80 cubic feet of compressed air. The underwater navigation events ranged from 700 to 1500 meters each. We'd exit the boat, shoot an azimuth with our compass to a specific spot on the shore while we were treading water (this time with our fins on our feet and some air in our BC!), then submerge to 20 or 30 feet and fin hard while keeping that azimuth. To pass the test we needed to be within about 20 meters of the target every time and within a strict time standard. Fast and accurate.

The third week we learned closed-circuit operations and underwater navigation and infiltration with a Dräger LAR 5 system we had on our chest. Drägers have re-breathers so that the air that you exhale is cleansed through a substance called DiveSorb, a lime pellet compound. The benefit with a closed-circuit or Dräger system is that there are no bubbles floating to the surface. With no bubbles a Dräger allows you to infiltrate and sneak up on the enemy.

We put it all together in the fourth week with a couple of tactical exercises down off the Florida Keys.

The Army scuba course is a truly great course. I was happy to get the opportunity to go. I was *especially* happy to have passed. It was absolutely the most challenging physical course I have ever done. It was more physically challenging than football, Ranger training, airborne training, and even Special Forces training. Add it all up and that work in the water was certainly the most unforgiving environment I've known.

14

Training for Unconventional War in Europe

When I was ODA commander in 10th Special Forces Group, the Berlin Wall was still in place. Like most of the rest of the military, we spent all of our efforts preparing for a potential war in central Europe against the Russians. Every few years, several of the ODAs were fortunate enough to participate with other European allied nations in what's called a "JCET," Joint Combined Exercise for Training.

As a detachment commander for a combat diver team, I was able to apply and get our team selected to attend a JCET with the Danish Frogman Corps. For one month in early March, we went to Denmark and to the Danish Frogman School scout swim course. It was a great course with lots of hard work and lots of cold-water swimming. The graduation exercise was a ten-kilometer swim. It literally takes all day to swim ten kilometers. We jumped in as a team and swam across a fiord with two- or three-foot waves of cold March water; we left in the morning and got to our destination that evening.

One of the exercises we did again and again was a series of long surface swims, one of them an infiltration swim with our gear on. On this swim, when we got to the objective, one of my team members looked at me and said, "Sir, I dropped my machine gun." Of course, on a maritime infiltration like that you have all your gear tied onto your body with a series of quick-release mechanisms so if for some reason you start going down, you can jettison your gear and still come to the surface and survive to fight another day.

In this case, the weapons we had were old World War II Stein guns. That is a 9mm submachine gun with the magazine out on the left side at 90 degrees from the pistol grip, the kind of weapon you see in the old World War II Resistance movies. The Danish frogmen used these during their training because they were pretty simple, easy to clean, and work well in and around the water. So when we got to the beach of the fiord in March, my team member realized he'd lost his submachine gun.

Well, we don't lose guns in my business. It simply is not acceptable. He generally knew where he lost it, somewhere about 200 meters out from the shore, paralleling along the shore the last couple of hundred meters prior to our objective. So we called the instructor over, got in boats, and went out along our swim course to look for the weapon. At this point the fiord was about 10 meters deep, so about 30 feet deep, and maybe 20 feet deep in some places. We started 100 meters out and we free-dived, all twelve of us, down to the bottom of the fiord, one at a time, for about two hours, but had no luck finding the weapon.

Lo and behold, just before I was about to call it quits and surrender this weapon to the fiord, one of my soldiers came swimming to the top with the machine gun in his hand. "I got it!" That's how we like stories to end.

Another exercise we did during this course proved to be particularly difficult. We had to free-dive down about 20 meters, or 60 feet, which is pretty deep, grab a bunch of seaweed from the bottom, come up, and show the instructor. The objective was to make sure the combat diver had the wherewithal to continue to the bottom, could control his breathing, and didn't blow his eardrums out on the way.

Just prior to that dive, one of my soldiers complained that he had some pain in his ear, so I had my Special Forces medic look at it. Sure enough, he had a badly bruised eardrum. To dive down to that depth with an injured eardrum would risk puncturing the eardrum which would be a lifelong injury. After discussion with the medic, and with that particular soldier, I made the decision not to let him make the dive. He was heartbroken. He was a brave soldier: "Sir, I can do it. I can tough it out. No problem. It'll only take a couple of minutes. I'll be fine." But the fact of the matter is it would have been a permanent, life-changing injury were he to puncture the eardrum. So we waited a couple of days and he later did it on his own. He wasn't very happy about that, but he did pass that test (as did we all) and he graduated from the course without damaging his eardrums. That kind of personal responsibility and motivation said something about the people I may one day have to count on to save my life.

Another task we completed in Denmark that spring was called *boat casting*. Boat casting is a means of infiltrating a dive team into an enemy-controlled area by simply jumping off the back of a fishing trawler or any type of boat as it sails along the enemy coast at night. The basic assumption is that all coastal countries have fishermen sailing around and a boat that sails without slowing down to offload anything, well, that's normal, and it would be hard for the enemy to know for sure if the boat was fishing or carrying an SF team out to infiltrate an objective.

There is some skill to completing this task — it is not simply jumping off the boat. The swimmer must face away from the boat as he jumps so his back slaps the water and not his face. He also has to learn to hold his body tight so as not to make a big splash. Of course, we had our combat equipment also, so we had to synchronize our actions — tossing the gear and then immediately stepping off ourselves — before the relatively short rope between the gear and our body became taut and pulled us overboard. We practiced this time and time again and at different speeds and in different water conditions.

Similar to this was another one of our exercises called *helo casting*. Instead of a boat, a helicopter flies several hundred meters offshore without necessarily attracting much attention. The key here is to keep the helo moving at its regular speed and not to lower it too close to the surface. We'd practice this flying at 10 knots (about 13 mph) and 10 feet above the water, then at 20 knots and 20 feet, then finally at 30 and 30. For the final evolution, we jumped off the bird at 35 mph and fell into the water from 30 feet. In helo casting, you must likewise face in the correct direction so you land on your back.

Both with boat casting and helo casting, successful infiltration depends on the craft's not appearing to be dropping anyone off. That means the faster the better, and never slowing down. (Ouch.) Of course, after getting our collective bells rung from several 30 km/hour jumps into the cold waters of the fiord, I was comforted to learn that this was the last option for infiltrating enemy-controlled areas. I'll get to the enemy and do my mission but I'm human": I'd be happy not to have to get to him this way. But the enemy doesn't wait for ideal conditions, so we trained for any contingency.

Just prior to our graduation I asked to see the school commander, the Danish Navy captain, along with our primary instructor, whom we called "Tarzan." Tarzan looked like you would expect a Danish Frogman to look: tall, blond, blue eyes and fit like ... well, Tarzan. We were all pretty excited that the team had made it; we'd all been worn out on a daily basis but we all made it! I was to report to the captain at 0900 that morning to talk about some graduation questions. The instructor and I stood outside the commander's hallway, as we looked at our watches and silently counted down 5 ... 4 ... 3 ... 2 ... 1 second to 9:00 o'clock. I knocked on the door at exactly 9:00 o'clock because that was the culture. 0900 means 0900, period, not plus or minus a minute.

This was one of the first times as a young Special Forces officer that I really got to work *by, with and through* the indigenous culture, in this case, that of the Danish frogmen. We learned how to earn their respect on their measures, against their standards, in their environment, and we had a really good time doing that. We focused on their heritage, their rituals, and what made *them* tick.

We'd run PT through the Viking graveyard, an area near their base in the woods that had large earthen mounds where they buried their old Viking kings, and we'd swim past Viking graveyards. These Danish frogmen were the last of the Vikings and their world was a Viking world, and we showed our respect for that. And the fact that we were able to persevere on their terms in their environment despite some pretty harsh conditions—that we had respect for their traditions and lived the way they lived—really gained us their respect and I believe taught me and the entire team the benefit of working with other cultures in their environment. That discipline has paid huge dividends for me over the years.

Tenth Special Forces Group is tasked to conduct unconventional warfare in Europe. Because of that, we conducted a lot of what we call *environmental training*. The environment that we focused on was the high European mountains in cold weather. For the four years of my first tour in 10th Group, we conducted a winter environmental training exercise in Canada every year during January, February, and March.

Now, as a Southern boy coming out of Kentucky, the largest piece of ice I had ever seen was in a mint julep. That is, until we went to Canada and we parachuted into the snow with a hundred pounds or so of gear in our backpacks. Then I saw lots of ice. I got up from landing on the drop zone and looked around and I realized that the entire world up here was frozen. My detachment and I were sleeping in snow caves, moving from point to point during the day, conducting operations, linking up, conducting long-range communications, conducting first aid, live-fire raids and a myriad of other tasks that make up this concept called unconventional warfare (UW). We conducted full training exercises in temperatures that approached forty degrees below zero. But that's what the Tenth Group was originally chartered to do—*unconventional* war. UW is what I grew up doing as a Special Forces officer. And what I advocate as the best way to win our current war on terror.

15

The First Desert War

In 1991, when the first Iraqi War broke out, Tenth Group was tasked to go into Northern Iraq and work with the Kurds. I'll never forget getting off the back of a CH-47 helicopter in the north in an area called Kurdistan; we were absolutely loaded for bear. Carrying as much ammunition as we could, plus our M4 carbines and our 9mm Berettas, we got off the helicopter and we all realized that we had gone back in time about a thousand years. I looked out across the mountain peaks and saw virtually no signs of modernity.

We flew in with the most modern technology available and the local tribesmen came up to us on horseback. The wind echoed with emptiness. Our mission was to work with the Kurds and help them get their lives back in order after years of having been horribly punished by Saddam Hussein. Saddam had gassed tens of thousands of the Kurds both before the war and after the war broke out, and they began a mass exodus to the mountains. You could see how desperate they were to flee. The road was littered with broken-down cars and all sorts of personal belongings that had simply been discarded and left behind. Our mission was to help the Kurds recover, to bring peace and a sense of calm back to the area. They needed food, water, medical help—just about everything. That was the first time I'd seen such abject sorrow and despair. I'd trained for it. But it still got my attention.

That's when I started to internalize this concept of unconventional warfare (UW). It's why an A-team is organized and trained the way it is. It's why Special Forces exists.

Tenth group deployed from our base in New England into an airbase at Incirlik, Turkey, where we staged for our entry into Iraq. Our battalion plan was to build three Joint Special Operations Areas, JSOAs, one for each company, each about 30 or 40 kilometers apart. We were a tactical force — light, flexible, mobile — so we didn't bring armor or artillery. The JSOAs would have three rings of security. The outer ring would be patrolled by the locals, the indigenous forces, or *the indig*. They knew everyone and would sense trouble long before we could. The medium ring was about three kilometers from the main base. It had observation posts and listening posts (OP/LP) and was patrolled. The inner ring was basically the end of the line. We had fighting positions just outside of our tents. You could roll out of your tent and into a fox-hole and that was it. We did not want to use the inner ring.

The 10th Special Forces Group commander at the time was Col. Bill Tagney, a great Green Beret and a good man. I've kept up with him over the years. He later became Lt. Gen. Bill Tagney, the deputy commander of U.S. Special Operations Command in Tampa. No other full time Green Beret has ever made it higher in rank. He was the first, and so far the only to make it that high. But during the first Iraqi War, he was the 10th Special Forces Group commander and also the commander of the Combined Joint Special Operations Task Force (CJSOTF) for that phase of the war. That's similar to the job that I had in Afghanistan some ten years later.

When my battalion, 3rd Battalion, 10th Group, deployed into Iraq in 1991, I was a young captain and the assistant operations officer for the battalion. I remember talking to the local Kurds trying to get the situational awareness that we needed. We were trying to figure out what they were doing, what the risks were and what the population needed.

My friend, the battalion intelligence officer, made a slip of the tongue. He was talking to the Kurds, stressing to them that America would be there forever, that we'd be there for the long haul. I quickly pulled him aside and said, "Hey, don't make those kinds of promises. We don't know that we'll be here forever. In fact, I'm pretty sure we're *not* going to be here forever. From what I understand, this is a fairly short in-and-out mission and we hope to be gone in two or three months. So be careful what you promise. It is obviously an exercise in patience and we want to make sure we don't raise false expectations from the beginning."

This phase was a humanitarian mission. The ground fighting in the first Iraqi war was over literally in just days and the president wanted to bring stability to the area. One of the things we did was to orchestrate the movement of the Kurds from Turkey back into northern Iraq. Now remember, conditions were terrible. These people had been abused and had almost nothing left, and this was a long refugee movement across rough terrain involving a lot of people. We set up a series of water and food way-stations heading from northern Turkey back into Iraq. I remember being at one way-station with several other SF soldiers, when a family came walking down the road and we gave them several gallons of fresh water. The father picked up a couple of cans, carried them away from our camp, and then made his wife and children carry the water so that he could walk ahead with nothing but his AK-47.

It suddenly dawned on me that this was a totally different society. Had that been an American family, the father would have loaded himself up with as much food and supplies as he could. But in this culture, the Kurdish and Iraqi culture, the women and the children carried everything and the father basically walked along the road with nothing in his hands whatsoever. Except, maybe, an AK-47.

Just before we redeployed back home, things had pretty much quieted down. A couple of our guys took some fishing poles down to a small lake to see what they could catch.

"What are you all doing?" one of the locals asked them through an interpreter.

"We're fishing," they answered.

"Here is how we get fish here," replied the Iraqi as he tossed a hand grenade into the center of the small lake. Fishing for sport or fishing for food; makes all of the difference in how you do it.

As a professional soldier, you notice the little things other soldiers do. I'll never forget: I was driving an M-151 Jeep up the little road by our camp towards a Kurdish camp in northern Iraq. Several Kurdish Peshmerge soldiers were walking along with their AK-47s. I gave them a ride. My friend and I drove up there with some six Kurds in the back of the Jeep. They put their AKs on the floor between the two seats of the old Jeep. I couldn't help but look down and notice that every single one of their guns was set on *automatic*. American soldiers are taught from the very beginning: keep your weapons set on safe until you're ready to pull the trigger and kill somebody. But Kurds, Iraqis, Afghanis and virtually every Muslim I've ever worked with overseas, habitually keeps his weapon on automatic. The perspective seems to be "if it is your time to die, you'll die and keeping your weapon on safe won't help."

We got along well with the Kurds. Wonderful relationships were built. One of my soldiers played a practical joke on one of the Kurds and I think everybody got a big kick out of it — except perhaps that particular Kurd. My sergeant happened to be dipping a bit of Copenhagen tobacco and one of the Kurds asked him what it was. He got out his tin and showed it to him and gave him a pinch, which of course they'd never had before. I can assure you that got his attention in a hurry. I believe that Kurd was sick to his stomach for quite some time after that. That probably was not the best way to build rapport, now that I look back on it.

The early UW activities of the first Iraqi War, when we began to infiltrate and work *by, with and through* the Kurds, really paid huge dividends with the more recent war to topple Saddam.

16

Staff Time

Shortly after I gave up command of my A-team, I went to the battalion staff as the Assistant Operations officer. As part of that assignment I went to a two-month school at Ft. Leavenworth, Kansas, called Combined Arms Service Support School (CAS3). It was a school where the Army taught mid-level captains how to become staff officers. I learned a lot of things at that school, including how the big Army thinks and how to staff operations and activities. The task our class was given was to put together a plan for a big battalion defensive operation for the defense of a piece of Germany called the Fulda Gap.

For the previous 20 or 30 years, our military assumed that if the balloon went up during the Cold War the Russians were going to attack the west by sending columns of tanks through the Fulda Gap. To defend against that, a huge portion of our Department of Defense assets were allocated to the Fulda Gap.

I went to CAS3 just after the Berlin Wall went down, so I was surprised and even annoyed to see that we were still training soldiers to defend the Gap. I got into an argument with my instructor, who was a lieutenant colonel (I was a captain at the time), saying, "Why are we defending the Fulda Gap? Let's get on with it. The next war's going to be in the desert. We know that the desert is producing an endless number of angry young Muslims. Let's get over the Fulda Gap and move on."

My words fell on deaf ears, of course, and we did our exercises and defended the Fulda Gap brilliantly. I have to admit, we did learn some good staff preparation, although it was hard to be enthusiastic preparing for the previous war.

As I gave a portion of the brief back to my peers, I erroneously used a term that drew a lot of anger from some of my classmates.

I was describing how one battalion would conduct a counter-attack while another battalion would be in the supporting position, and then how all the administration for those battalions would be back in a safe rear location.

The term I used for that safe rear location was where the "clerks and the jerks" would be. As I looked out across the classroom, I realized that several of my classmates were in fact "clerks and jerks" and didn't appreciate that comment. Up until then I'd never really worked with anybody except combat arms, paratroopers, Rangers, and Special Forces types. I assumed that is what our Army was made of. Well, we all learn.

Overall, I had a great time at that course. I could not get motivated to spend a whole lot of time studying the Fulda Gap, but that course still allowed me to pick up a skill that would become my next passion in life. Nowadays, after my family, which comes first, and soldiering, which is a close second, I have a real passion for horses, something I owe to the Fulda Gap. One evening after class I went to a local stable near Ft. Leavenworth and I said, "Hey, I've got some extra time. I'll be here for about two months. I'd like to learn how to ride a horse."

The instructor said, "Okay. What kind of riding do you want to do?"

"Well, I want to learn the fancy kind," I said.

"What do you mean *the fancy kind*?" he asked.

I said, "The fancy kind. Not the kind with the cowboy saddles but the other kind. The kind with the other saddles."

"Oh, you want to learn English riding?"

I said, "Yeah, exactly. I want to learn that kind."

So I took classes two or three nights a week for the next month or two. It turned into a love of horses that's been a part of my life for the decades since and eventually grown into the passion of fox hunting (chasing foxes with hounds while on horseback). Wherever Mother Nature takes that fox, you follow as fast as the cagy fox wants to go. If the sport was good enough for George Washington and George Patton, I figured I should check it out. Glad I did. Even after having been to war a couple of times, I will admit that some of my highest adventures have been while fox hunting!

I have to smile because my first few riding classes consisted of this tough Green Beret captain and a bunch of 12-year-old girls. But we all dutifully obeyed, walking in circles as the instructor yelled at us to keep our heels down, our shoulders back, and our hands out front.

The instructor eventually let me take another class with adults. That class was full of 40-year-old housewives. At one point he yelled, "Imagine your favorite movie star. Everybody picture your favorite movie star." So along with all those housewives I pictured my favorite movie star.

And he said, "I want you to ride this horse like it was your favorite movie star. Wrap your legs around this thing like it was your favorite movie star."

And I looked at him and I said, "What?!?!"

And he looked at me and said, "Who's your favorite movie star?"

I said, "John Wayne's my favorite movie star." They all got a good laugh out of that.

When I got back from CAS3 to my battalion, I took command of Support Company for 3rd Battalion, 10th Special Forces Group. I loved it. I had the mechanics and all the cooks and supply sergeants for the battalion in my company—a little different from commanding an A-team. A lot different, in fact, but still a challenge and an honor. Every Friday morning, we did a company run. I'd lead these young guys through the woods, across creeks and over jumps that I'd set up for my new horse, a retired steeplechase racer who did not know that he was retired. The men thought I was crazy, but we were not just soldiers—we were airborne soldiers, so we needed to be fit (and perhaps a little crazy), and those runs created a common bond for the whole company.

But I'll never forget my supply platoon sergeant, a senior soldier who'd been in the army probably 12 years or so. He was a sergeant first class in charge of the supply and maintenance platoon. He refused to go to airborne school. So I talked to him and said, "Hey, Sergeant, you're a platoon sergeant in an airborne company. You have to go to airborne school." Still, he refused, so I told him to go find a job somewhere else on post. I was through with him and I relieved him of his position.

Of all things, he filed an EO complaint with the post Equal Opportunity office. He claimed I fired him because he was black. That began a huge investigation. The entire chain of command investigated my company to see if it was in fact racist or bigoted. Composition-wise about a third of the men in that company were black, two thirds or so white, with a few Asians and Latinos mixed in as well. At the end of the day, the investigating officer agreed with me that as an airborne company, black or white, you've got to be airborne qualified if you're going to be a leader in the company. No grounds for any kind of equal opportunity complaint. Our biggest complaint was that this platoon sergeant was a bit of a knucklehead. The day he went somewhere else was a good day for me.

One of the great things I learned as the Support Company commander was the tactical aspects of logistics. I learned how to manage and account for millions of dollars worth of military gear, from trucks to mess halls. I signed for everything.

By "signing" for a piece of equipment, a vehicle, a weapon or weapon system, the signer personally takes fiscal responsibility for it. He or she must ensure all of the pertinent parts and pieces are there when he gets it, and again when he signs it over to the next user. A commander does not sign for every piece of equipment individually, but on an all-inclusive hand receipt.

When a new company commander takes command of a company, whether it is a Special Forces company or a quartermaster company, he or she conducts a detailed inventory of every piece of gear in that company. In most commands, the new commander must "sign for" that gear before he or she takes the unit's colors. If that commander is smart, and most of them are, they will have every piece of individual gear signed for by its user before they sign the overall hand receipt.

Company commanders and below sign these hand receipt rollups. Battalion commanders and above ensure their subordinate commanders manage their property properly. As a captain and major, I signed for three separate company hand receipts in the three times I got to command a company, entailing several million dollars' worth of government equipment, vehicles, weapons, field gear, office equipment, computers, you name it. I am proud to say that, when I signed the equipment over to the next commander a year or so later, in every case I was able to account for all of it. Some commanders have to pay out of pocket for any gear lost on their watch.

When I took command in Afghanistan, the supply, maintenance, and accountability process was much more complicated because we had a combined *and* a joint task force, so each nation and each service brought their own gear with them. I did not sign for anything other than my own personal weapon and field gear, but I was responsible to ensure my subordinate commanders maintained what they had, and more importantly, I faced the challenge to ensure they had what they needed.

When I left my first tour in Special Forces after four years, I'd commanded an A-team, I'd commanded a support company, and I'd gone to war in the first Iraqi War. I was loving life. The Army assigned me to Personnel Command in Alexandria, Virginia right across from Washington, D.C., to manage the personnel assignments of various officers, most but not all of whom were Special Forces.

I was there for one year and it turned out to be the longest year of my career. The woman I sat next to was a civil servant, fairly junior in grade, I guess, but way junior in motivation, I am certain. Every day she would start off the day saying, "I'm so tired. I'm so tired. I'm so tired." After a couple days of this, I put my head on my desk and almost cried, saying, "How did I get to this? Two months ago I was commanding an airborne company and now I'm stuck on a desk with this crazy woman."

I did learn several important things during that tour. I learned how the Army personnel system works. The Army is about people. That is the currency we deal in. It's not tanks. It's not airplanes. It's not ships. It's people. I learned how people are evaluated, how people are assigned, and how people are promoted to support our Army and its important mission.

I also learned that America has two Armies: one Army that fights and overcomes the enemy, and another of accountants and clerks that fight for the resources we need and then allocates those resources in accordance with some big spreadsheet. I was fortunate to spend the vast majority of my 24 years in the Army that fights for a living, although I now know the great value of the other Army as well. The week I left the Personnel Command was a great one. I left that office, got promoted to Major (a year early), and Ann and I had our first child, all in one week. That week was hard to beat!

17

Unconventional Warfare as Illustrated by Tom Sawyer

After years of studying and training as an unconventional warrior, it hit me that the real definition of unconventional warfare is one we all read about in the 8th grade. That's when we read the book *Tom Sawyer*.

You'll remember that in Mark Twain's famous book, young Tom was tasked in the first chapter by his aunt to whitewash the fence. Well, Tom did not want to whitewash the fence himself, so he conducted *unconventional warfare*. He got all the neighborhood kids involved. He motivated them to want to whitewash the fence. He taught them how to whitewash the fence. He gave them the equipment to whitewash the fence. Then he supervised them as they whitewashed the fence.

At the end of the day, the fence got painted. Everybody on the street had bought into the idea of taking care of that fence. Everyone was proud of what they had accomplished — that fence was now *their* fence. In military speak, young Tom had acted as a force multiplier: he was a leader using the premise of unconventional warfare, which is accomplishing your goals by working *by, with, and through* the indigenous population. Tom Sawyer is the best example of unconventional warfare that I've ever seen. He got the locals inspired and motivated to take on the task themselves. That's what we unconventional warriors do.

When I took the colors of the Combined Joint Special Operations Task Force in Afghanistan, I simply tried to repeat the lessons of Tom Sawyer. I prayed every night for two things: (1) for the wisdom to lead these soldiers as they and our nation deserve to be led, and (2) for my family's safety and well-being while I was gone.

I deployed to Afghanistan from "Green Ramp" at Ft. Bragg, North Carolina. While excited and honored to get the opportunity to lead soldiers in the Global War on Terror, that day at Green Ramp was a sad one. Ann and our two daughters were there to see me off. My girls were young and had not yet really grasped the concept that I'd be gone for an extended period. I hated to leave them. I'd never felt a pain like the pain in my heart when we waved goodbye.

The flight over took almost 36 hours, with a couple of stops and one in-flight refueling. I went into the cockpit to see the refueling operation. We were flying at about 30,000 feet somewhere over the Republic of Georgia under a full moon. The KC-135 refueler lowered a giant gas boom with small wings on the end and maneuvered it to the vicinity of the C-17 pilot's windshield. Then the C-17 made some final adjustments and the boom operator on that big tanker plugged the fuel cap right above the cockpit. At 30,000 feet, flying about 300 mph, at night, on the

KC135 from the Alaska Air Force National Guard refueling the C-5 filled with Green Berets on the way to war, about 30,000 feet somewhere over central Europe; great to be an American!

far side of the globe, the U.S. Air Force had brought together two giant airplanes into a formation where the planes were just a few feet apart in the sky, right where they needed to be, right when they needed to be there.

It is good to be an American in this day and age.

My goal was to combine that level of technology with a unique and unconventional way of fighting our war — Tom Sawyer goes high tech. And nowhere would the lessons of Tom Sawyer be more readily apparent than in the fifteen or so Special Forces "A" camps we had scattered around the country of Afghanistan.

Afghanistan is about the size of Texas, or, for those with a more global perspective, slightly smaller than Germany. Running through the middle are the rugged, 24,000-foot Hindu Kush Mountains. Around the perimeter of the country is the only major network of roads. "Major" is a relative term. At its best, it's a two-lane highway. A poor nation with few raw materials, Afghanistan has been at war for 25 years. About three-quarters of its people are illiterate. Most will never go to a movie theater, eat a Big Mac, see a stoplight, or, most importantly, even see a real doctor. In the past 50 years, they've gone from a monarchy, to a communist dictatorship, to utter chaos, to an extremist Islamic state. Now they're fighting for something called "democracy."

A major player in Afghanistan's recent history was the Soviet Union, which attempted to run Afghanistan with a puppet government from 1979 to 1989. During that period, the Russians systematically destroyed what little infrastructure the country had. They also killed 1.3 million citizens and ran about three times that number out of their homeland into refugee camps in Pakistan.

After the Soviet withdrawal in 1989, the leadership vacuum was eventually filled by the Taliban government. "Talib" means "student." The Taliban government was impoverished, uneducated, and angry at their treatment by the Soviets. Under the Taliban, women were not able to attend school, walk in public without being covered and escorted, have a job, or in any way choose their own fate. During my year in the country, I seldom saw an adult Afghan woman's face.

The exile of such a large number of Afghans into the refugee camps of Pakistan changed the very fabric of the once close-knit societies of the Afghan tribes and villages. Of course, it was this chaos of an uneducated, impoverished, and angry society that allowed the terrorist organization Al-Qaeda to use Afghanistan and its Taliban government as a safe haven to train their terrorists and to plan the Sept. 11, 2001, attacks on the United States.

18

The Lware Campaign

Our main effort in Afghanistan involved the use of Special Forces "A-camps" that we had placed around the country. Now first let me tell you that we called them Special Forces A-camps because they were camps from which an ODA team, an Operational Detachment Alpha, could project its power. As I said earlier, A-teams project their power through unconventional warfare by focusing their efforts *by, with and through* the indigenous population. Those three words— by, with, and through — are the key to how you see things as an unconventional warrior. We did not call them "fire bases" from which we projected firepower, nor did we call them "patrol bases" from which we deployed unilateral combat patrols. They were A-camps, from which we projected unconventional war efforts: *by, with and through.*

One of these A-camps we had was placed in an area called Lware (pronounced "L-ware"). Lware is the district along the Afghan — Pakistan border. About a year or so before I got to Afghanistan, shortly after early America operations in Afghanistan began, there was an A-camp in Lware, but it constantly came under fire from the Pakistani border and the Taliban and Al-Qaeda that crossed that border. So for whatever reason, the American leadership decided to close that camp down.

After we were there and gained some SA (situational awareness) about what was going on, we realized that the Lware Province had become a sanctuary for Al-Qaeda. With the mountains and ridges going east-west as the border went north-south, there was a natural flow for people to walk from Pakistan through the Lware Province into more central Afghanistan. And Al-Qaeda used that same flow for its movements, making Lware an Al-Qaeda sanctuary.

A major part of our strategy in the Combined Joint Special Operations Task Force was to focus this war *by, with and through* indigenous populations. In order to do that, no matter what the situation, the answer is giving the indigenous population the tools to execute the solution themselves—having them pull the club out of the bag and use it properly, to use the golf metaphor. Not me, not us; *them*. Whether you're building a school, building a road, gathering intelligence, or conducting a raid, the best answer is to somehow help the indigenous—in this case, the Afghans—build that school, build that road, gather the intelligence, and, ultimately, conduct the military operation against the terrorists. Everything should have an Afghan face on it, not an American face.

In the Lware Province, after we realized it was an Al-Qaeda sanctuary, we gave an unconventional warfare mission to one of our Special Forces A-team commanders. I told him basically, "I want you to move into Lware Province. I want you to bring stability. I want you to take as many Afghans as you can muster and I want you to get ready to go as soon as you can. What are your questions?"

The young detachment commander and his eleven Special Forces A-team members spent about two or three weeks gathering intelligence and coming up with a plan. They put together an indigenous team of warriors and also brought with them the heavy weapons section from the Afghan national army, including three Afghan mortars that were really old Soviet 60mm and 82mm mortars.

Again, the main effort of this operation was to work *by, with and through* the Afghans in the Lware Province, not to move in with 300 Americans, but to move in with a handful of Americans and a couple of hundred Afghans and to set up an Afghan border checkpoint. That's unconventional warfare. Put an Afghan flag on it and arm it, equip it and man it with Afghan soldiers and Afghan police officers.

As the plan began to unfold and the team began to conduct their analysis, I gave them a bundle of cash to pay the Afghan customs guards who hadn't been paid in a while, thus beginning to warm the locals to the idea of democracy. One of our sayings was that while you cannot *buy* Afghan loyalty, you can *rent* it, which is better than not having it at all.

The ODA did their leaders' reconnaissance several times before they began their movement into Lware Province. Deploying a force creates a particularly vulnerable time while they're en route to their destination,

These men proudly fly the national colors on their gun truck. The vehicle is armed with an M2 .50 cal and an M240B 7.62mm machine gun. More importantly, the vehicle is manned with Green Berets ready for unconventional war.

so we use everything we have to stay alert to the situation. Using a myriad of technological and professional tricks of the trade, the A-team was able to identify an enemy force as they began to move into position.

So the A-team commander stopped his convoy. He quickly sent a couple of Americans around the edge to sneak up on the other side of that mountain. They had orders to take out the Taliban if they were getting prepared to initiate an ambush on us. That's one of the few times when it was right to do a unilateral U.S. operation — that is to use force, quickly, violently, and decisively. But this one had to be done properly, without drawing attention to our assistance, so we wouldn't water down the main effort, which was this unconventional operation *by, with and through* the indigenous capabilities.

The A-team came around and sure enough they saw the Taliban in place for the ambush. My men took decisive, unilateral action, and it was a short, one-sided firefight. We won, they lost. Cost us bullets, cost them blood. This is a good example of a successful execution of unilateral combat operations to support UW (unconventional warfare) operations. We were able to pre-empt that ambush on the Afghan and U.S. forces, who were thus able to continue on in their movement toward the new camp.

When they got there, they began to set up our security and equipment at the Lware A-camp, also called the Lware border checkpoint. One of the first things that they did was to place the Afghan infantry company with an Afghan flag proudly flying on the hilltop. It soon became obvious to the enemy that these soldiers, Afghans, were here to stay. They weren't just passing through, as had been the case for the last year or so.

They had with them trucks, they put up tents, they dug foxholes, and they began to emplace things called HESCO barriers. HESCO Barrier Blast Walls have been in use by our military as a quick and easy way to provide base security since the 1991 Gulf War. HESCOs are large wire baskets about six cubic feet that you put on the ground, unfold and then fill up, using a front-end loader from a tractor, with rock and dirt and gravel. So, ultimately, you have a wall of HESCO barriers around the camp, which is much like an old fort or castle from medieval days.

As the CJSOTF Commander of some 4,000 troops, I found it was no longer possible for me to go on all of the combat operations personally, as would have been the case when I was a captain or major in command of a much smaller force. Not only were there too many operations like this, but I knew I had good men running them, and a constant shadow from "the colonel" would undermine their authority.

Instead, I picked the ones that were most significant and tried to be there to spotlight their successes. I knew that as the joint force commander my presence would focus the rest of my command on what this team was doing and, in fact, I could focus the eyes of the entire joint task force on them.

So on the day after our A-team set up their new camp in Lware, I flew out with my command sergeant major and my radio operator to spend the night with them. I wanted to see for myself what was going on, but I also wanted the rest of the joint task force to see through my eyes what was going on. This was a major operation involving a few of us working through a large-scale deployment of Afghans. This was how this UW concept *should* work.

My command sergeant major, Tom Reese, my communications sergeant, Master Sergeant (Big Jim) Haddock, and I flew out there in a Black Hawk helicopter. As always, we had an AH-64 as the accompanying gunship.

When I left my headquarters in Bagram on a weekly basis it was in a helicopter or in a convoy of just a couple of SUVs. Most of my vehicles were civilian SUVs of all types— Land Rovers, white pick-up trucks; I even had a Cadillac SUV — all of which had been absolutely beaten to hell. When I'd fly out via a chopper, I'd walk or convoy the half mile or so to the chopper pad.

My headquarters and the airfield were all within the same secure perimeter. I'd carry my body armor even though I was still in safe country. When I left my compound, I hadn't yet locked and loaded until after we loaded the Black Hawk and took off. My commo sergeant had a constant SAT Comm (satellite communications) capability so I could reach back and talk to anybody I needed. He had all the encryption devices needed, so that's all done via secure. I also traveled with my command sergeant major, Tom Reese, who traveled pretty much everywhere with me.

I always had a map in my pocket. I had my own personal survival radio in case we got shot down or separated from each other in an evasion scenario. I also always carried a "basic load" of 5.56mm ammunition for my M-4 carbine. A basic load consists of six 30-round magazines plus a magazine in the weapon. I also carried an M-9 Beretta with its basic load, which in my case is four magazines plus one in the weapon for a total of 5 magazines of 9mm ball ammunition.

Any time I left my HQ, I was armored up and wore a Kevlar helmet with a night vision scope receptor, and then the night vision goggles themselves under my shirt on a rope around my neck. So at night I took them out, snapped them into my helmet receptor so that the goggles clicked down over my eyes, allowing me to see. I had a couple of canteens; I'd typically keep the map in my cargo pocket and a survival knife on my belt. Combat ready.

Now, having said that, everybody in Afghanistan locks and loads if you're outside of the headquarters compound, or "outside the wire." Probably half the military who served in Afghanistan or Iraq seldom left Bagram or Kandahar or one of the big camps in Iraq. They never got outside the safe perimeter so there was no reason to lock and load. I was out every couple of days at least, usually for several days at a time. So I was locked and loaded almost the entire time.

The round is chambered. You only take the safety off when you're ready to pull the trigger and kill someone. You never move with the safety off, even in a firefight, until you have the target in the sights. It's a final step but it takes a split second to shoot somebody after that. I'd lock and load both weapons, my pistol and M-4, every time I left the perimeter. As soon as the helicopter flies away from the camp, lock and load. Or as soon as you drive out of the gate. Or in my case, right before I'd drive out of the gate, because a lot of bad things happen at gates. There's a large congestion of civilians who are unvetted and allied soldiers. The enemy thinks of one of our gates as a target-rich environment.

The two senior sergeants I traveled with were equally equipped every time. We had backpacks with sleeping bags and a couple of days of emergency rations. My communications sergeant had a satellite radio with a primary and alternate set of batteries, and a big satellite dish which looked like a reverse umbrella. His rucksack was heavier than most, probably about 100 pounds, a significantly heavier rucksack than the one I carried. Our body armor was a light body armor with heavier plates over the chest and back. There were many different styles. The style I had was basically a vest with large plates on front and back. Then I had a lighter, inner body armor that I put on underneath, almost like a T-shirt. Then the vest had pouches sewed onto it for the ammunition magazines and canteens, so it was all-inclusive.

Then we got on the Black Hawk as I did two or three times a week for a year. I put the headphones on so I could talk to the pilot. We had a door gunner typically on both sides. And we had another bird flying shotgun, an Apache gunship, an AH-64. We never had one bird flying alone — always had a wingman. Always had emergency search and rescue capabilities. When one bird goes down, the other bird supports and calls in fire and continues to fight.

The support offered would depend on which bird goes down. If an AH-64 goes down, the Black Hawk can land and get the other crew. A gunship wouldn't be able to pick everybody up if the Black Hawk went down. But they would be able to provide fire support and call in another helicopter. So we would take off and as soon as we crossed and left the airfield, everybody locked and loaded their weapons. The door gunners locked and loaded their M-60 machine guns mounted in the doors of the Black Hawk, the passengers locked and loaded our own personal weapons, and at that point, it was game on.

The route was not a straight and flat route like when you fly Southwest or Delta from Washington to Atlanta. Army choppers pretty much try to fly nap of the earth, which, as the name implies, is flying along the contours of the earth, up and down the valleys until they get to the series of mountains, and then they typically go up real high. One of the challenges is that gunships and Black Hawks can't fly over the summits of a lot of the Hindu Kush Mountains. So when I flew in a Chinook CH-47 because of its higher altitude capability, I would fly over the big mountains. We flew east through the valleys for about an hour or so until we got to Lware.

Whenever we flew, I constantly looked over the map and out the windows trying to keep situational awareness of where we were. In case you get shot down or crash, you always want to know where you are. It is real easy to get lost if you find yourself in the middle of high mountains in a fiery crash. Even if you can't find your way out, the enemy can always find you because of the smoke and explosions of a crashed aircraft.

On my body I had a compass as well. I wore standard desert camies (camouflage) with my dog tags laced in my boot. That is a lesson I learned long ago. If you get killed in action, and your head gets blown off, they've got your tags in the boots, and thus can identify the body. I've actually had soldiers killed who lost their dog tags because they were so violently injured. Luckily we knew who they were. But it's just a personal thing you learn along the way. Even to this day if you come out to my farm, you'll see dog tags in the laces in my work boots.

Whenever we left Bagram we would leave in sterile uniforms, meaning no patches, no insignia, no tags, no rank, no nothing. I had the pin-on rank of a colonel, an eagle, in my pocket so that if I was talking to somebody I could have it pinned on, or I could also take it off, depending on who it was. I never wore my name tag when talking with the indigenous. They didn't need to know who I was by name. My soldiers knew who they were talking to. Locals didn't need to know the specifics except that I was the boss.

Whenever we landed in Lware, of course I'd be on the headphone talking to the pilot, and he'd point out various things on the way into the LZ. We both make mental note of various things for later reference. For example, keep an eye out for that ridge line, look at the distances to the closest cover over here on the left.

Frequently we'd see mirror signal reflections on the peaks. That's a very efficient, and almost impossible to stop, technology from a thousand years ago. There's only one reason for a mirror to be signaling on the top of a 14,000-foot mountain: that reason is to notify someone that helicopters were coming.

Also along these mountain ranges we would see stacks of rocks, tall and thin like a human, stacked six feet tall, one on top of the other. From a distance it looks like a human standing up there. And again that's part of the ruse that the Taliban had learned from the war with the Soviets, lessons learned from their big brothers in many cases: build man-size rock stacks just to keep the enemy guessing. If it looks like there are people standing along the ridges, it makes you think twice. Again, ancient technology, but you still look twice.

We had the most advanced technology on earth, but several stacks of rocks, stacked man size, and a few boys with mirrors on the hilltops, would make us react to them, give them the initiative. So as we flew over the village of Lware itself, our camp was probably 300 meters or so to the east between Lware and the border. My rule was not to put any camps within 3 or 4 kilometers of the border: we had to have some operational maneuver space, so if we got punched we could counterpunch.

We were not allowed to cross the border because American forces crossing into Pakistan would create an international incident. That was absolutely the right answer. Even if that was not the Joint Task Force policy, I would have enforced it myself. The Taliban was begging for us to cross the border into Pakistan. Because if we crossed the border, Pakistan had no choice but to defend its borders. That's what countries do. They defend their sovereign borders. So we were very careful about not crossing borders in spite of the tempting offers to kill Taliban waiting on the other side. We got permission to be closer to the border than the conventional forces. I think they had a 10-kilometer buffer. We got it down to 3 or 4 because we had different people with a different mission. I did not want to cede those extra 6 or 7 clicks (kilometers) to the enemy.

19

Firefight

At Lware, the Black Hawk would land as the gunship flew circles. The gunship started flying those circles around the LZ even before we landed to exit the Black Hawk. The AH-64 Apache flew a kilometer or so in every direction, looking. It was basically an M-230, 30mm chain gun with a four-blade, twin-engine helicopter built around it. The purpose of the attack helicopter on these missions was to keep the Black Hawk safe. A pilot and copilot were the gunners, fore and aft, with the pilot sitting behind and slightly above the gunner.

The Apache typically would accelerate about 2 minutes from landing and get to the landing zone 30 seconds prior and just do a quick air recon, fly a couple of laps around it, make sure we had security on the ground, make sure they didn't see anything fishy. If they had, the gunner had his finger on the trigger, ready to go.

My pilot called ahead prior to landing to say that "Bushmaster 6" was going to land at 2100 Zulu. Incidentally, our watches were always set to Zulu time, which is Greenwich Mean Time. Whereas most countries have an hour differential between time zones, Afghanistan has 30 minutes. When I first landed in Afghanistan I said, "Hey is it 9:00 or 10:00 local time?" And they said, "It's 9:30." Afghanistan is never quite in sync with the rest of the world.

So the Apache did an aerial recon around our A-camp. We landed. Command Sergeant Major Reese, Master Sergeant Haddock and I disembarked and were welcomed by the ODA commander, who in this case was a warrant officer because the battalion was short of qualified captains. This team didn't have a captain so the executive officer was the commander. This A-team was from the Florida National Guard and they were awesome. Good leadership, very capable, just good guys all around.

I learned long ago that ultimately leadership is what makes the difference, and this National Guard A-team is a great example.

We got there in midafternoon, and I did what commanders have done for a thousand years. I tried to quickly gain situational awareness of the battlefield. So we walked the perimeter of the camp. We walked up to a couple of the LP/OPs (listening posts, observation posts) on the peaks overlooking the camp and also overlooking into Pakistan. It took about an hour to walk to the LP/OP. It's a pretty significant hike. The camp itself is probably about 7,000 or 8,000 feet above sea level and the LP/OP is probably about 1,000 feet above that. Carrying body armor, basic load, rifle, pistol, and helmet — a climb like that is a decent little athletic event. It'll get your attention. The Afghans were walking along with us with AKs and a magazine in their pockets. They all appeared to weigh 140 pounds or so.

It started to get pretty hot. In the afternoons probably in the 90s — it's pretty toasty. This was March 5 — still spring. But we were working up a pretty good sweat. We got up there and sat around with the LP/OP crew — talked to them about what they were doing, about where they had their antipersonnel mines, their fields of fire, and what they see as the most likely avenue of approach for the enemy.

I had a pretty good methodology, having done these battlefield circulation tours every few days for a year, and less often for the 20 years prior to my Afghan tour. I started by basically just asking questions — the kind of questions that make the soldiers and their leaders think about the right answers. Simple Army questions: Where's your field of fire? So at night when I can't see out there, I know that I go from this rock on my left to this rock on my right. That's my field of fire. And you literally have rocks or aiming stakes in the ground right up here by the gun. At night when it's confused, you can't say, "I'm aiming at that hill," because you may not be able to see that hill. But you can say you're going to kill everything from that aiming stake on the left to this aiming stake on the right. The guy on my right has the next aiming stake from here to there. And those stakes are literally right in front of the guns.

That is the sort of questions I asked a thousand times. And in many cases I was talking to Afghan soldiers. So the questions were pretty basic. My soldiers had night vision glasses and thermal imaging devices, and more importantly, years of selection and training. So it was a little different with the Afghans, who didn't have any of those things.

We tried to have interlacing fields of fire. Mutually supporting fires, so that the enemy is not fighting against 300 individual men, but against one strong position. Each man supporting the one to his left and right, no matter what. This is the same tactic that good armies have focused on back in the days of the Spartans. So I walked around the Afghan companies' positions.

They'd only been there a day, so they were still at the early onset of defensive position improvements. But I learned as a young lieutenant in Ranger school that position improvement and security never ends. It starts as soon as you get someplace and continues until you leave. We put that into practice on a regular basis.

I did not need to give a lot of tactical insight or guidance because in most cases, and certainly in the Lware A-camp, the ODA commander and his weapon sergeants and operation sergeants were experts in both the art and the science of unconventional war. They knew exactly what they were doing. But the fact that the old man was coming to check always made people pay a little closer attention.

Across the AOR (area of responsibility) for the entire Joint Task Force (JTF) and the Combined Joint Special Operations Force (CJSOTF) as well, we had all types of weapon in place for various uses. One was the claymore antipersonnel mine. The claymore is an extremely powerful weapon.

American soldiers set the claymores with great caution. They are directional, but the back-blast area is lethal up to about 20 or 30 meters, so you have to place them far enough in front of your position to be safe for the user. It's more lethal in front, with a killing distance of up to 100 meters, but it's still lethal to the rear of the weapon. A claymore in most front yards would blow out all of the windows across the street.

Named for the legendary Scottish sword, a claymore has a layer of C-4 explosive and about 700 steel balls like BBs, about the size of #4 buckshot. These are packed in a cigar-sized, convex green plastic box. In classic "GI-proof" packaging, the box has "front towards enemy" printed on it. The LP/OP at Lware had a couple of claymores.

I saw some of the local workers lining up for work. This was a signal that this camp was here for good. As soon as my team got there they brought with them a truck full of HESCO barriers. We brought maybe 200 or 300 HESCO barriers and put them in a huge circle. We had a couple of container boxes in the center, for the A-team headquarters, and then a ring of HESCO barriers around the team HQs, and then foxholes and gun positions external to that.

The camp itself was on the top of a knoll with low ground all around it, but with higher ground and higher knolls out past that. Then there was the small village at the bottom of the knoll next to it. The village of Lware was 200 or 300 meters to our west from our knoll-top A-camp.

Pakistan was to the east. We knew that's where trouble was coming from, so that's where our main focus was, although there were certainly some auxiliary underground members in the village of Lware. The guerrilla fighters were coming from Pakistan, thus that was where most of our weapons were aimed.

Like every other camp I visited, at Lware, I got a tour, talked to all the soldiers and got a good idea of what was going on. What I like to do is get the senior leaders or sometimes the whole A-team together and just kind of tell them the strategic view of what's going on from the old man's perspective. More importantly, I'd listen ... from the tactical view, what was going on from their perspective.

What I always tried to do before my tour in Afghanistan was to skip an echelon, go from my echelon, past the battalion, sometimes past the company to the A-team. That would do a couple of things. One, it would give me a "no kidding," ground truth understanding of what's really going on, good, bad or ugly. And two, it would give them a "no kidding," ground truth about what the boss's intent was without any filter.

As an aside, it allowed me to check the company battalion headquarters to see how much information was getting filtered one way or the other. More than any commander wants to admit to, ground truth information somehow gets filtered out as it flows up or down the food chain.

I had common talking points at all these camps. As I got to Lware and we did the security tour and I got the leadership together, I started discussing these talking points. We got our MREs out and I'd just ripped off the top of my pork patty and my jelly and crackers and started talking the point that the kind of effort I saw here at Lware is exactly what we needed to do.

Point number one: "The default answer to every question is to get the Afghans to do it." The Lware A-camp was the strategic tip of the spear for my number one point, not only because the A-camp was in an enemy sanctuary, which was good, but because there was an Afghan flag up there, not an American flag. There were two Afghan companies and there was an Afghan border checkpoint. Real countries have border checkpoints with their own soldiers and their own flag. People in Lware didn't even know Afghanistan had a border patrol. Now they had one right there with an Afghan flag.

The default answer to every question is: get the locals to do it. No matter what you want done, get the locals to do it. We may have to help them. We may have to pay for them. We may have to mentor, cajole, threaten — doesn't matter. While in the middle of that first talking point, brilliant speech that it was, there was a loud explosion followed immediately by gunfire.

We were sitting around on ammo cans, folding chairs, jerry cans, whatever we could find handy. I was talking with a couple of officers from the A-team and the Civil Affairs and PSYOP (psychological operations) teams that were attached to the A-team there. My frequent battlefield circulation was imperative to get a realistic view of what was really happening and what could potentially happen and I wanted to get their thoughts on how we could grow UW from tactical to strategic success, from a couple of camps like this one to the entire nation. We were just getting ready to open up the rest of our MREs (meals ready to eat) and have dinner in the rocky hills of eastern Afghanistan at about 7,000 feet above sea level. Before we could open our rations, we were interrupted by a loud explosion which initiated what turned out to be a deadly, 45-minute firefight. Forty-five minutes is a pretty long firefight for a counterinsurgency in this kind of scenario.

The firefight was initiated by two Special Forces soldiers posted on an LP/OP, a listening post/observation post, on a hill overlooking our camp, which also overlooked the route from Pakistan into Afghanistan. Our camp was about three or four kilometers from the Afghan-Pakistan border and from the hilltop, our observation post could see the path through the valley that the Al-Qaeda and Taliban would walk as they came into Lware. So we armed up a couple of SF soldiers with sniper weapons and, of course, their small arms and placed them on top of that hill to see what was going on. We reinforced the area around them with a claymore landmine.

Those two heroic Special Forces soldiers at the LP/OP saw about two dozen well-disciplined soldiers coming from the east to the west, coming from the Pakistan border toward the Lware A-camp and assessed that the enemy was well disciplined because they moved in good wedge-shaped "V" formation. There appeared to be about 5 to 10 meters between the two wedges, they had their weapons at the ready, and they were communicating via hand and arm signals, which indicated to us that they were men who had some Al-Qaeda training, rather than some local ragamuffins that were walking ducks in a row, straight line, nice and close like untrained Taliban sometimes did. These men were well disciplined and well trained. Al-Qaeda.

As these two wedge formations came down the valley, the point man of the first wedge held up his arm to stop. He knelt and looked down right in from of him and saw a wire running along the dirt. Well, the wire happened to be connected to that Claymore land mine. He picked up the wire and followed it with his eyes up the hill and the last thing he saw was a blond-haired, blue-eyed U.S. Army Green Beret sergeant looking at him holding the "clacker," or the initiator, for the Claymore land mine. Our sergeant initiated the land mine; it went off and vaporized the first couple of terrorists in that formation just as it had been engineered to do. About ten minutes of fierce fighting ensued, involving rifles, small arms, and hand grenades.

The two sergeants circled back to the A-camp and organized a platoon-sized patrol from the Afghan infantry company to go up in there and try to chase out the Al-Qaeda. They were a brave, determined force. In the meantime, we returned fire with our small arms and the mortar sections.

Now, just as a personal coincidence, with my radio operator, Master Sergeant Jim Haddock, who had traveled with me all over Afghanistan — a great American — I jumped into the first foxhole that we came to when the bullets started flying. Half of this bathtub-sized foxhole was shared with an Afghan mortar section consisting of two Afghan soldiers. The two Afghan soldiers had with them an M1942 Soviet 60mm mortar, M1942 indicating that it was designed in 1942. So, pretty old technology. Still, the simple mortar worked. The Afghan soldiers were not firing that mortar, possibly because they hadn't identified the exact location of the enemy, or perhaps because they weren't told to do so, or because they were not familiar with the weapon.

Master Sergeant Haddock and I, however, knew that the enemy was east of us, so *we* started firing that mortar. We set it for maximum charge and low elevation, which gave it a maximum range of about 1500 meters. We were firing past the LP/OP with the intent to simply keep the terrorists' heads down and have them rethink this assault on the Lware camp.

After the forty-five-minute fight, we ended up calling for air support. USAF B-52s were on station flying CAP, combat air patrol. By the time the B-52s were there and ready to drop their bombs, the enemy did what the Al-Qaeda does best: when they come up on a force that's bigger and stronger, they simply disappear. But that's okay. Because the force they came upon was an Afghan force with an Afghan infantry company fighting under Afghan colors. That signaled to them that the *locals* were in the fight, *not just* Americans, who would someday pack up their gear and go home. The Taliban who escaped would tell their commanders that they had fought the Afghans. I can tell you, those Afghans were mighty proud to win that firefight, as proud of themselves as I was proud of the way the whole engagement came off.

All explosions feel different depending on the proximity and the size. The Claymore's explosion was a couple of hundred yards away so it didn't shake my soul. I didn't feel a thump in my chest like what I've felt in other occasions in Afghanistan, Kosovo or on the training ranges back home. It was smaller because the claymore itself only has about a pound and a half of C-4. As soon as we heard it, we figured it was a claymore.

Typically, IEDs, which are the most common explosion for combat soldiers in the current war, have much heavier amounts of explosives. They also rely on the target moving, not being stationary. We knew we had no friendly forces on the move around our camp. Rockets fired in have more explosives than a claymore as well. I heard a lot of those. This didn't sound like that.

I've heard a lot of claymores in training, but that was the first one I'd heard in combat. The explosion was followed immediately by gunfire. We heard the gunfire of two distinctively different types—7.62, which meant AK47s, and 5.56 and 7.62 from the American rifles. So we heard the explosions of the gun itself about 200 or 300 yards away and then in a few seconds we heard the rounds start to go by our heads.

We did the same thing that soldiers have done for thousands of years. We dropped our MREs, we donned our helmets—I'd taken off my body armor, so I quickly put it back on. We donned our gear and tried to immediately gain SA (situational awareness). It was just starting to get dark, probably about 1900, 7:00 P.M. local time, or about 1230 Zulu. The ODA commander and I were sitting together. He knew the area better than I did, of course, because it was his camp, and he'd been doing reconnaissance missions there for about a month. He said, "That's our LP/OP. They're just on the other side of that ridge and it sounds like a claymore." We heard more gunfire going on the other side of the ridge. We had a gunfight at the LP/OP. Now everybody was thinking the same thing. We had two guys—two Americans, two SF soldiers—one ridgeline over, in the middle of a pretty significant gun fight.

In this case, 200 or 300 meters over a pretty steep hill, so a fair piece. We don't have eyes on them but we're hearing it. And we can tell what's going on —claymore and guns, multi- caliber, multi types.

In about three minutes we transitioned from eating MREs, fat, dumb, and happy, to quickly putting on our gear, and then rounds started coming into the camp, inbound rounds. Outbound rounds you can hear the report first, and loud. Sometimes with inbound rounds you hear the rounds first (which sound like popcorn) and then you hear the report, depending on how far away the weapon is. Not really loud, not like what you see on TV. Popcorn and then dust kicking up around us.

The Afghan National Army soldiers were in their foxholes, which they had just dug the day before — by the way, this is rock, so they're not much of a foxhole.

The SF weapons men got on a Humvee. The ODA commander and his gunner got on a Humvee with an M2 .50 Cal Browning machine gun on it. The M2 (called "Ma Deuce") was designed in World War I. It is still simply—awesome. It shoots a projectile about the size of your thumb with a maximum range of about 2,000 meters—incredible weapon!

They drove the vehicles around the corner of our little valley so they can see up that valley towards the LP/OP. It's got the M2 .50 Cal and an M-240, 7.62 machine gun as well.

So, within just a couple of minutes, some serious lead was going downrange in support of our little 2-man LP/OP.

We were laying down what is called "suppressive fire." Not terribly accurate, but meant to keep the enemy's head down and reduce their movement. My sergeant major, communications sergeant and I kind of went from where we were eating dinner to the military crest of a small hill. The "military crest" means we're on "this side" of the hill enough so that we're protected by the hill but we're on top enough so that we can see over it. We were on a small hill, maybe five feet. It just so happens that there was a foxhole with a mortar in it and an Afghan National Army mortar team. This foxhole was the size of an American bathtub, maybe.

The Afghan soldiers weren't firing their mortar because nobody told them to fire their mortar. Bullets were still flying all around us, kicking up dust. What we'd identified, from my position up the hill in front of us on the left, was that the LP/OP was in the middle of this running gun battle. Also in front of us and to our front right were two Taliban crew-served machine gun emplacements that were bearing down on our camp from probably 500 or 600 meters away and at a higher elevation.

At that point, we were hearing the popcorn, dust kicking up all over, our .50 Cals opening up pretty good, Afghan soldiers starting to return fire, although it was suppressive fire because they couldn't really see what they were shooting at. My sergeant major was next to me and he was supplying some suppressive fire too with his M-4 carbine. My communications sergeant, Jim Haddock, had been my como sergeant for about eight months at that point; the sergeant major had been there maybe a month or two by that time. Both great guys, smart, hard as nails and good honest men; America's best. So Haddock and I looked at each other, then at the Afghan mortar crew, and the mortar crew was not firing.

By sheer coincidence, I had learned to be a pretty good mortar man when I was a lieutenant. Pretty simple technology. The mortar is a tube with the firing pin at the bottom. You drop a round down the tube; it slides onto the firing pin. The pin ignites the fuse, which ignites the propellant, which shoots the round back up the tube to the target. Hasn't changed much in almost 100 years. We climbed into this foxhole. I said, "Jim, start passing me ammunition. Take them out of the box and pass them." We just kind of crouched over to the hole because we were on the military crest, protected to some extent. The mortar itself was on top of the hill. So we walked around and we sat on the ground with our feet in the foxhole. It was so shallow, our feet were on the bottom of the foxhole. It was only a foot and a half deep. And the mortar men were sitting next to us, not really doing anything, but I didn't speak Pashdo and I didn't have an interpreter with me.

Jim began to unpack ammunition from the almost antique Soviet wrapping. He kept them on max charge and started handing me rounds.

A sixty-millimeter mortar is of course sixty millimeters in diameter, side to side, passing through the center of the round. Say about the size of a small coffee thermos. The projectile itself is about as big as your hand. So the whole round including the propellant is maybe from your elbow to your knuckles if you make a fist. At the opposite end of the round from the projectile there are what we call cheese charges. They are the explosive propellant that shoots the mortar up into the air. The more propellant, the greater distance it goes. If you want to shoot it close, you take off propellant, or the cheese chargers. You have charge one, which is one charge, then charge two, charge three, charge four. Max charge is every slice of cheese (propellant) that comes in the packet; for this particular round it was charge four. Mortars, much like hand grenades, have a safety pin in the nose of the actual projectile that goes downrange. So you pull out the pin just like a hand grenade, you unwrap the packing material around the cheese charges—that's what the assistant gunner does.

That's what Jim Haddock was doing. He'd open the canister, which is a cardboard cylinder with black engineer tape around one side, rip off the tape, take off the top of the cylinder, let the round slide out. He'd take off the packing material around the cheese charges, all the paper and cardboard, pull the safety pin, hand it to me. I was the gunner. I'd hang it in the sixty-millimeter mortar tube. The weapon was a tube probably about a foot and a half, maybe two feet long with a base plate about the size of a dinner plate to keep the tube from burying itself and drilling a hole into the ground. Then towards the top of the mortar tube were two bipod legs each about eighteen inches long.

It can be *direct laid* or *indirect laid*. *Direct lay* is when you look and eyeball where you're shooting. *Indirect lay* is where you lay multiple mortar tubes parallel so they are laid together. Then one of them has an aiming circle with a particular elevation and quadrant so that all tubes are laid on a particular line. If you know your target is exactly 1427 meters on an azimuth of 93 degrees magnetic, you can then lay all the guns that way with some pretty sophisticated algebra and get steel on target. You look at your tabulated firing tables—TFTs—to see the charge required for, in this case, a 1400-meter firing mission. That's called mortar gunnery for indirect lay.

We had no time for mortar gunnery. We were direct laying the gun. I was on my knee looking at the tube, holding it in my hand saying, "I know the LP/OP is slightly to my left. I can see the far line of our troops right in front of me and the enemy is past that." So I told Jim, "Give me max charge, one round." I hung the first round, it slid down the tube, hit the firing pin at the bottom — thump!— there's the explosion and I could see it traveling through the air, generally in the right direction about 1500 meters downrange.

That was a little bit too far. I wanted to bring it in a little closer. So I elevated the tube, aiming more "up in the air," thus heightening the elevation of the round and shortening the distance traveled. I had no levels or bubbles on that 1942 weapon. I just used some good old Kentucky windage. I did it again and it was a little bit closer. I didn't want it too close because then I'm shooting my own guys, who are about 200 or 300 meters in front of me. Certainly didn't want to fire to the left because that's where the LP/OP was. I don't know exactly where they were because they'd certainly moved out of their original position. So I gave them 300 or 400 yards of safe maneuver space.

I found what I thought was a pretty good protective fire location, about 200 or 300 meters beyond the far line of my troops and a good 300 or 400 meters to the south of where the LP/OP was.

And then Jim started unpacking rounds as fast as he could. The rounds themselves were probably older than I am. When you're firing mortars, there are very directive weapons safety procedures. For example, if you have a misfire these procedures are pretty rigorously followed in the American Army. The procedures are different for a hot tube than they are for a cold tube. What you don't want to do is set the mortar down with a hot tube and then the hot tube slowly heats and cooks off and explodes the cheese charges in your hand and then this thing shoots out right in front of you. But at this time, with popcorn going on in my ears, dust kicking up around, one round didn't go off.

So I knowingly violated the very directive U.S. Army weapons safety procedures. I turned the mortar upside down and put my hand down over the tip and let the mortar slide back out of the tube. I looked at it and realized that Big Jim hadn't taken the safety pin off. So I took the safety pin off, threw it at him, hung it again and we fired about 25 more rounds.

I did stop halfway through and put my gloves on because I couldn't hold it anymore; the tube was too hot. And again, I was always aiming well south and well forward of friendly positions, so this was strictly harassing fire to keep the enemy on their toes.

By this time after just a few minutes of the fight, we had the .50 Cal on the Humvee putting some pretty good lead downrange. We had the Afghan soldiers who were starting to return fire pretty seriously, and now we were dropping mortars on the enemy. So the enemy was thinking twice: "Okay, this is not going to be as easy as we thought. We can't just kill them while they're eating dinner." We had 200 or 300 soldiers, counting the Afghans and the Americans, and they were putting some pretty serious return fire out there.

This continued for about 45 minutes. The weapons sergeant on that team was Sergeant First Class Nathan Dallas, who coincidentally was in my battalion when I was a battalion commander at Ft. Carson and in the Ranger Regiment before that. He had gotten out of the regular Army and joined the National Guard, and lo and behold, was with me again. He got the American 60-millimeter mortar, a much more modern and capable weapon than the Soviet 60mm that I was using, and he started shooting up illumination rounds because it was starting to get really dark. At this point the enemy quit firing.

So we ceased firing to regroup and see what was going on. I told Jim Haddock to get the SATCOM up so we could call in the Sit Rep (Situation Report). He was already setting it up. Again one of the reasons I was in Lware was that where I went, I knew the attention of the Joint Task Force went as well. We sent 300 Afghans and a dozen or so Americans out there for a purpose, to fight by, with and through. It took Jim a couple of minutes to get the SATCOM up and going. He checked our communication link because there's about a two second pause between when you click and when you get a click back. That's the line of sight from the antenna to the satellite and back. That's called a ping. So we got a ping, he gave me the handset, and we were on the air.

I did something that I learned to do as a cadet back around 1980 and had done a few times in training as a lieutenant. But the task I was about to perform had really gone out of vogue with the onset of digital instant communications.

I gave a verbal SALUTE report. The acronym SALUTE — size, activity, location, unit, time, equipment — was an Army standard until about the late '80s and '90s when nobody spoke on the radio anymore because information was mostly passed via digital messages, not voice. A SALUTE report, I learned thirty years ago, I could do in my sleep. So I called my headquarters to give them a SALUTE report because that's the fastest way to get the point across. Not a big narrative — just one sentence each for size, activity, location, unit, time, equipment.

Just before we got our radio up and going the two soldiers from the LP/OP came back to camp. They told us what they had seen from their perspective, which was that of two Special Forces sergeants, behind camouflage, looking over this valley that overlooked the route into Pakistan with a claymore anti-personnel mine probably 100 meters in front of them.

So they looked out from their LP/OP and they saw two wedge formations of about a dozen or fifteen men. A wedge formation is a V formation: a man at point, a couple on his left flank, a couple on his right flank like a V, a reverse V. And then, behind the first, was another identical wedge formation.

That tells you a couple of things. It tells you somebody trained them. And it tells you they're fairly disciplined. They were giving hand and arm signals and they were spread out so that one gunshot or one hand grenade would not kill two people. What that also tells us is that they were either Al-Qaeda or trained by Al-Qaeda. They weren't just some angry locals, walking like ducks in a row to go shoot some Americans. They were on a mission. They had rehearsed it. They had a command and control set-up. And they knew what they were doing.

The first guy stopped, looked down at the ground, and picked up the wire that goes from the M57 Firing Device or "clacker" that the observation team had in their hand to the claymore that was camouflaged under some brush. The wire looks like a wire for an electric light in your den or bedroom. Except it is olive green. The point man for the first wedge formation picked up this wire and he followed it with his eyes all the way up toward the top of the hill. I can only imagine the last thing he saw was an American with sparkling blue eyes and blond hair. He must have just seen that Green Beret and his clacker. The American squeezed the clacker, thus initiating the claymore that was a foot and a half behind the bad guy. He was vaporized. The couple of guys right next to him also went down.

The LP/OP, in this case, was armed with an M-24 sniper rifle, which is a 7.62 mm rifle with a night vision scope on it. One of them had an M-4 carbine. They both had M9 Beretta pistols and hand grenades and of course, the claymore. The sniper took out two or three more bad guys with his M-24. The M-4 gunner, the spotter, picked out two or three more.

At the end of the day about nine or ten terrorists were killed with a sniper rifle, a carbine, pistols and, hand grenades and of course, the claymore. If you're close enough to throw a hand grenade, you're pretty darn close. Our LP/OP was on a hill. The bad guys were probably 50 to 75 yards in front of them, a pretty significant 2-way firefight going on. These two SF troopers let off a barrage and killed about 8 or 10, turned around and slid down the reverse slope of this gulley.

They moved out of the LP/OP area and made it back to the camp,

200 or 300 meters behind. By the time they got back to the camp, the rest of us had been in this thirty-minute firefight, mortars, machine guns, M-2 .50 cal, Afghans firing ... a pretty serious firefight for this kind of war. They came in and gave me and the ODA commander a good debrief about the details. They had all their sensitive items and weapons with them. They wisely left their rucksacks with sleeping bags and chow.

At this point it was dark. Jim looked up and said, "The SATCOM's up, ready to report." So I got on the radio and gave them this SALUTE SITREP that I learned in 1979. My call sign was Bushmaster 6, my headquarters was Bushmaster. Call signs are numbered by your position. Six is always the commander. So anywhere in the world if you hear someone on the radio that says this is something "six," that's the commander of whatever organization that is. Third Special Forces group is called the bushmasters, for the poisonous African snake, and Bushmaster Six is the group commander. On a joint staff like mine in the CJSOTF, the J1 is the personnel officer, the J2 is the intel officer, the J3 is the ops officer, J4 is the logistics officer, J5 is the plans officer.

I got on the radio and I said, "Bushmaster three, this is Bushmaster six,." knowing full well that at my headquarters, my JOC, Joint Operations Center, they had the radios manned 24/7, huge maps all over with the various units and staff's representative there 24/7 from the J-one, two, three, four, five all on the table, and they were tracking the battle. What I wanted them to know was that we had a firefight and we had fast movers inbound and I needed them to know the situation.

So I gave a SALUTE report: Size — Approximately 15 soldiers; Activity — moving from east to west in two wedge-type formations; Location — 300 meters east of Lware A-camp; Unit — appeared to be Al-Qaeda or Al-Qaeda trained; Time — 1300 Zulu; Equipment — AK-47 and machine guns. Appears to be 10 enemy KIA, no friendly KIA or WIA. Two flat tires on the HMMV, no other damage. All friendly accounted for.

The radio operator at my headquarters was Bushmaster 3 Tango, meaning the J3's radio operator because the J3, LTC Joel Woodward, wasn't sitting next to the radio; he was in his office on the other side of the room "Bushmaster 6, this is Bushmaster 3 Tango. Stand by, Bushmaster 3 is on the way." It's funny because the radio operator is probably

23 years old and he'd never really worked a voice call before. He'd been in radio communications his whole military career (about 5 years) but he hadn't done many voice transmissions like this. He'd probably never heard of a SALUTE report. It's something you read about in the history books. They don't teach it anymore.

But my J3, Lt. Col. Joel Woodward, who is now a colonel in the regiment, an outstanding UW officer and a truly great guy, knew what a SALUTE report was. Joel got on the radio and said, "Bushmaster 6, this is Bushmaster 3. I'm prepared to copy." So I gave him the SALUTE report.

On the other radio, the ODA commander had already called in fast movers, jets that fly close air support. There was a CAP, Combat Air Patrol, overhead all night, every night, some kind of American warplane flying overhead. And whoever gets in a fight calls them and they come to you. So when we called, the USAF came to us with the closest thing they had in the air. Afghanistan is a pretty big country, so it probably took them 30 minutes to get to our little corner of it.

It happened to be B-52s that were on CAP that night. That is modern war. The biggest, most capable bombers on the planet, looking for a dozen riflemen deep in the mountains. Couldn't see anybody to drop bombs on, so we really could not use them. Had we been able to use them, they would have been great. The CAP had our A-camp location because our location was entered via GPS back at the headquarters. So it wasn't just Col. Herd's map-reading skills; they knew exactly where we were.

We called in the SALUTE report and spent the rest of that night on a pretty high state of alert, which means about a third of the team was up manning various positions. A third of the Afghans were up too, so that meant 33 percent alert status, which is higher than usual. My sergeant major and como sergeant, Jim Haddock, and I slept on the west side of that big steel container box, also called a "connex," that acted as the A-camp HQ. It was fairly chilly that night, I remember. But I slept well. The next morning we got up and surveyed the battlefield a little bit.

We looked for the dead but couldn't find them. Muslims typically take their dead back home right away. We had pretty much searched the kill zone, which was about 300 or 400 meters out from our camp. So sometime during the night they came and picked them up and dragged them back. Muslims believe it is important to be buried within 24 hours of death. So they were under the ground, I'm sure, by the time the sun came up, or close to it. My guys picked up their sleeping bags, etc. Jim Haddock at breakfast went over to the mortar and came back and said, "Hey, sir, there's a bullet hole in that mortar." I said, "Really!" So I went over and looked at it, and sure enough, where the bipod legs attach to the mortar, a little bracket had been shot off, which I didn't even notice at the time. That was a pretty close call.

The concern in this kind of war, both strategically and tactically, is that the enemy can always see us, but we can seldom see him. At Lware, we knew generally where they were. I couldn't see the enemy. Nobody really could see them except the two SF troopers on the LP/OP, and they killed about ten of them.

What we realized later was that the enemy was coming along and placing three guns overlooking our camp. They had placed the first two and were putting the third on the hill where our LP/OP was when our soldiers initiated their ambush. Had we not had those SF soldiers on that hill, the enemy would have gotten all three guns up there, and then they would have begun the attack as opposed to our beginning the attack. It's always better to start the attack. So the next day we went up there and found the gun positions from the other two guns but couldn't find any dead bad guys. Their guns were gone. We just found shell casings.

As soon as Americans set up HESCO barriers, the enemy knows we're staying. If you're just passing through you don't bother with the HESCO barriers. But if you're coming to stay you bring your defensive perimeter gear like HESCOs. Of course, the time for the enemy to attack is not after the Americans get their defenses set up, but before. The enemy did not know our intention until that first morning when we began to set up our A-camp. The most likely time for an attack in that scenario is the second night, which is why I got there on the first full day. I knew that was the highest risk level for our guys.

Two of the SF soldiers from Lware got Silver Stars, the two on the LP/OPs. Their courage literally saved the camp and the lives of several of their comrades.

The rules of engagement vary somewhat depending on where you are. But at the end of the day, if you are threatened, you must engage the enemy. And I would tell my people deliberately—and I would tell this to everybody that I visited in A-camps and every commander that I got to know—I said: "If you are threatened you are not *authorized* to return fire, you are *required* to return fire. Do you understand the difference?" And the SF guys got it. That's never a problem with a Green Beret. Those two great Americans on the LP/OP that night fired as soon as they had positively identified the men walking down that small valley as the enemy. Their call saved the lives of others and further propelled the cause of democracy in a corner of the world.

And they understand the concept of discriminatory fire, because they're very mature. Some ¾ of the men who try to earn that Green Beret don't make it. The ones who do have rehearsed it for years. That means you discriminate as to where you shoot. You don't just kick down the door and spray the room. You shoot this target, but not that target. So you discriminate. When it comes to firing weapons, discrimination is imperative.

That's why with 18- or 19- year-old infantrymen, they're very cautious about putting claymores out there because something bad might happen. But with 28-year-old Green Berets, it's not really an issue. The rules of engagement are such that if you are threatened, you return fire. Of course, if you're fired upon, you return fire.

The Afghans did a great job. My men did well, too. At the end of that firefight, my two soldiers had killed about ten of the terrorists with claymore land mines, sniper weapons, pistols, and even hand grenades. In spite of some of the bad things you hear about the American youth of today, our nation still produces some great young men, American soldiers!

20

Fire Support

Years before any of us even *knew* of Lware, let alone where it was, I was becoming familiar with the fire support capabilities we had for our Special Operations soldiers deep in enemy territory. A CAPEX, a capability exercise, is a show of what we could do as a military force. We usually only did them about every six months at one of the secret training facilities at Ft. Bragg for key leaders in Congress or the Office of the Secretary of Defense.

I still remember the words that I called over the radio one night as a young Ranger lieutenant at a capabilities exercise at Ft. Bragg, North Carolina. That particular night, we had Rangers and some of the other members in the direct action community doing the exercise. We had a target illuminated with infrared light and we called in a 105mm howitzer from an AC-130 gunship flying above.

I was the Ranger fire support officer. "Spector Gunship, this is Ranger Forward Observer," I said on the radio, which was plugged into a public address system for the VIPs to hear. "You are cleared hot to engage targets." I remember we brought the fire in very close to the spectators, the VIPs, so that they could really feel and smell and see what Special Operations soldiers do with that AC-130.

The AC-130 is a fairly old platform, very simple but very efficient. It has a C-130 Hercules chassis with some extremely high-speed electronics and three weapons systems. In the back left jump door is a 105mm howitzer, very similar to a 105mm howitzer that artillery units use. Forward of that howitzer is a set of two 40mm Bofors guns, and then forward of that is a set of two 20mm cannons. These three weapons systems are all laid parallel and all in sync with a series of computers inside the AC-130 fire control system.

20. Fire Support

The gunnery crew of the AC-130 is sitting in the back looking at a computer screen and they can see images and targets on the ground. They move the cross-hairs on the screen over the targets, then pull the trigger. The appropriate weapon system more or less explodes in a fusillade of shells as it engages the targets on the ground.

The AC-130 always flies somewhere between ten to twelve thousand feet above the ground in a left-handed circle so the guns are always aiming toward the ground. As a lieutenant, I had the opportunity to fly in an AC-130 gunship, and actually be the guy in the back shooting the 105mm howitzer straight down from ten thousand feet into the targets on the ground. I got to see the computer screens in the back where the gunners were moving their cross-hairs across so they could take out targets with 20mm, 40mm, or 105mm weapons systems from ten thousand feet.

One of the advantages of being that high is that the target on the ground can't hear or see the aircraft. So if you're a Taliban fighter on the ground — fat and happy, having your tea and rice, huddled around a small campfire in the middle of a cold, dark night — above you, these guys on this AC-130, using their infrared camera capability, can see in extreme detail how many people are around the fire, see what's for dinner, check out their weapons, and make a decision that could really spoil their day.

The AC-130 is the favorite fire support system of an unconventional warrior. It allows our Green Berets to get out there virtually on their own in very small numbers and get to know and work with the locals, yet at the same time, have U.S. Air Force technology only a radio call away. On many, many occasions, my SF soldiers would call up and say, "I just made contact. They ran off to the north." And the AC-130 on the radio would describe exactly what's going on. "I see two people running to the north. They just crossed the creek. I see three more people that are running to the northeast through a grove of trees. And it looks like two or three people hiding behind a building just to your south. The ones to your south have crew-served weapons. The ones to your northeast have small arms. And the ones to the far north have no weapons at all."

That's the kind of intelligence we can get with the AC-130 that makes UW really possible, because it allows our soldiers to go out there on a limb and still get back.

21

Returning Fire

America and the western world follow the concept of reciprocal use of force. That is one of the principles inherit in our laws of war. I don't agree with this as a blanket rule. Around 400 A.D., St. Augustine wrote a thesis on *jus in bello*, justice while fighting a war. As part of his just war theory, he argued that using disproportional force was wrong. I don't agree with the absolute use of the principle of reciprocal fire on a strategic or moral level, nor do I agree on a tactical level. When carried to its ultimate end, the theory of reciprocal fires would drive you to a scenario that if we are fired on by two guys with an AK-47, reciprocity would be 3 or 4 of our guys with similar weapons returning fire.

One time I had some explaining to do was at one of our A-Camps along the Pakistan border. That camp was named after an early American casualty. We had two A-teams and a B-team in that camp. We got some pretty serious indirect fire one night.

That particular A-camp had an airfield and hosted a dirt airstrip capable of STOL (short takeoff and landing) aircraft. I never saw a C-130 land there, but the runway was probably C-130 capable. I always got there via helicopter. Like all airbases in Afghanistan, this one was a former Soviet base. The runway was littered with probably 20 or 30 old and useless abandoned Soviet aircraft, just kind of pushed over there with their big red stars and all. I always got a kick out of seeing these Soviet transports lying cockeyed, wings on the ground.

The airfield had a couple of permanent buildings made out of bricks. "Permanent" is a relative term; with their sun-dried bricks, one good rain would wash away half of the buildings in the country. Of course, they seldom got one good rain. We added a couple more buildings made out of bricks and lumber. We occupied the whole airbase, which was probably fifty acres. It wasn't much. It was one runway of packed dirt with a building in the center of it just to the side, with a couple of little outbuildings next to that. We had an SF company and a couple of A-teams, a B-team, and two or three dozen Americans there as well as some indigenous soldiers. I went there frequently for a couple of reasons. One: it was a great camp with great soldiers running great combat operations based on sound intelligence. They were able to do this because they worked well with the locals. Two: it was from there that I checked on several border checkpoints.

When the Soviets left the country, they left hundreds of thousands of 122mm rockets that go in their rocket launchers. Since there's no retirement program in Afghanistan, the wise Afghan caches ammunition for his retirement to take care of that rainy day. Everybody who's anybody has a cache in weapons. A lot of people turned them over to us when the Americans came in, some just left them where they lay, thinking peace is here so I don't need them. Not the Taliban. The Taliban collected a lot of them. A lot of them are still out there. We found them all the time.

Because there is so little money to move society along the way to the future, the locals use this ammunition like Americans use their bank accounts to fend off the hard times. "Don't mess with him because he has 100 rockets. If you mess with him, one of them may be coming this way." These 120 mm rockets are designed to be fired out of Soviet BM-21 rocket launchers, of course. While many of the launchers are still around, they are fairly complex to fire and to maintain. In fact, what the Taliban would usually do is prop the rockets up with a couple of rocks and then generally aim them where they would want them to go. Then they would light a fuse or in most cases use an electronic ignition to launch it. It would hit within 1,000 meters, give or take, of where they wanted it to go. So it's certainly not accurate, but very common. It's a great area weapon and the runway at this A-camp provided a tempting target, apparently. I was rocketed at that camp one night while I was there. The base was rocketed several times.

By coincidence, two or three weeks later the camp received enemy rockets simultaneously in a very tight sheath. It was very unusual to get that many at once and they all landed together. Either someone had a rocket launcher or they had a homemade aiming system of some kind to get the rockets to land in the same place. On that night, about a dozen enemy rockets landed in a very close sheath, meaning very close together. Rather than one or two fired at random and landing here or there, these rockets were fired with precision.

But to get a dozen to land in close proximity in about a fifty-meter circle, that's some pretty good shooting. This particular night several rockets landed in a close circle about 75 meters right in front of the gate of the A-camp, meaning all the enemy had to do was add a bit of elevation to the rockets and they would walk right into the center of the camp. Not a pleasant thought. And that made the attack a real problem. They all landed about 50 to 75 meters from the front gate, right at the front door. So the company commander, being a smart guy, an SF officer, realized that all the bad guys had to do next was click it up about two clicks, raise the elevation, increase the range 50 or 100 meters, and the next salvo was coming in on his lap.

The company commander immediately called CAP, Combat Air Patrol, to see what was above and how fast they could get close air support. He knew the enemy had eyes on his camp and that they were feverishly working to raise the elevation enough to bring the next group of rounds right onto his head.

That night, the closest CAP happened to be an Air Force flight of B-52s with J-DAMs on it. The Joint Direct Attack Munitions is a guidance mechanism that converts "dumb bombs" into smart, laser-guided bombs. They are used for precision attack on fixed targets. The company commander identified the probable launching site from where the rockets came and they cleared the Air Force pilots to drop the J-DAMs. We dropped about six or eight J-DAMs. They cost about $100,000 apiece. We dropped about ¾ of a million dollars' worth of munitions on what was probably two or three Taliban, maybe 16 years old, running around in their man-dresses up in the mountains.

I had to justify that expense to the commanding general. He said, "You know we just spent about a million dollars of ammunition." I said, "Yes, sir, I know that." So I described the fifty-meter sheath about 75 meters in front of the front gate and the two clicks on the enemy adjustment knob that would bring the next round of fire through the front gate. There was no time to wait.

He said, "Well, you're right. I understand."

He did understand. It doesn't take long to click a rocket launcher's knob twice. I am certain that the men of that company thought that was the best million dollars they had ever spent.

But the rocketing stopped. Ironically, five minutes after the B-52 dropped the bombs, the next group of aircraft were en route: two Apache helicopters, which would have been much more effective. And the JTF commander kind of gave me a hard time about dropping J-DAMS at about $100,000 apiece. Had we known the Apaches were a couple of minutes out, we may have waited. But you never know. The commander absolutely made the right call. I would have done the same thing.

Was it overkill? Yes. Was it reciprocity of force? No. Are our men alive? You bet. So J-DAM was the right answer. He got the point. And a good point. We fired several hundred thousand dollars into a rockpile. But you never know.

Most rocket attacks were at night and when they came in, we soldiers did the same thing every night. Everyone put his combat gear on and went to his position. The weapons sergeants would man the mortars or the machine guns on the corner. The intel sergeants and the team leader would stay together and command oversight position. Medics would go wherever they needed to go. Everybody had a position on the wall. When I got to a camp, one of my first questions would be, "What's the plan if we're under attack?" Usually the commander would say, "My place is up there"—he'd point to one particular location— "because I can see and I've got communications so I can make calls if need be."

At this camp they had concertina wire around the outer perimeter and then strongholds around the building. So that's where we went, just around the building.

The night that I was rocketed there, I went to the tower with the company commander. We had night vision goggles and we were looking. We didn't see anything. The rockets were usually harassing fire. What the Taliban would do a lot is pay somebody ten bucks to go up in the mountains and shoot these rockets, then go home. No American casualties, no Afghan casualties, just harassment.

One night along the Afghan-Pakistan border, some of my soldiers were ambushed. They returned fire but the enemy had disappeared, as was frequently the case. Our soldiers were not wounded in the ambush, so it could have been much worse, but we did have that AC 130 over their heads almost instantaneously. They were able to follow the enemy soldiers, the terrorists, as they moved away from our location up into the woods. So over the next few minutes we were able to track them and see how many there were and what they were doing.

Now from my command headquarters at Bagram, my JOC, joint operations center, with its big map and a series of TV screens, we were able to track this whole battle in real time on the radio. When the appropriate time came and the ground commander requested fire support, we could either hand off that fire support to them for use at my subordinate commander's approval or we could authorize it ourselves.

On that particular night, from the airplane, they were following this mule train with about six or eight mules, going up a mountain trail at about 2:30 A.M. local time, and they appeared to be heavily laden. Now, mule trains, particularly heavily laden mule trains at 2:30 A.M., mean just one thing to us—logistical supply trains for Al-Qaeda.

So you have a mule train going away from an ambush site a half an hour up into the mountains. After a little discussion, the SF company commander on the ground near the ambush zone authorized the AC-130 to engage the target. The gunship killed all the animals, killed anyone in the area.

My soldiers went back the next morning, and found the animals right there. As it turned out, all of their packs had been cut off and the things that were in the packs had been taken — even the tack on the mules had been stripped off. Now interestingly enough, in this case, we received no complaints from the local villagers about killing mules. In every other case, if we hurt their livestock or hit a vehicle or anything else had been damaged in a firefight, the locals came to us saying America owed them money for the goats, chickens, vehicles or whatever.

But in this case, with six or eight dead mules, nobody came up and said we owed them money for the dead mules. Al-Qaeda. These mules were a terrorist supply transport; they'd helped in the ambush against my men, and they were up to no good. We were able to make that call based on the AC-130 gunship and the crew and the interfaces that we'd developed over the years between those airmen and our Special Forces soldiers.

I sat there in my command and listened to these conversations over the radio and could picture in my mind exactly what they were looking at from that airplane because I'd been doing that kind of thing for twenty years. Fire support plays a huge role in allowing the Special Forces soldier to get out beyond the conventional army's reach. That ability to provide covering fire and indirect fire to the Special Forces soldier when, in many cases, the SF trooper is the only American within 50 miles, really mitigates some of the risk of being out on your own deep in enemy territory. If worse comes to worst, an SF trooper can call in various types of fire support to allow him to break contact with the enemy and safely escape danger. We get a lot of that fire support from the Air Force with their AC-130 gunships or, occasionally, from a fast mover, a jet. We did have, also, some artillery pieces at the various camps and some large mortars.

COL Herd with the Afghan National Army commander for the region near Gardez. This photograph was taken in an ancient castle said to be over a thousand years old. The castle keep was full of 120mm Soviet rockets.

One time, I was spending a couple of days with the A-team near a camp in Gardez. There were two 105mm howitzers from the 25th Infantry Division artillery stationed there and they were conducting what they called an *artillery raid*. What that means is that they'd take these guns via helicopter pretty deep into enemy territory, drop them off so they could fire a few short fire missions real fast, pick them up, and then take them elsewhere.

While I was there, the howitzers were firing a mission called "direct lay," which means they were literally aiming their guns right into the side of a mountain about five or six kilometers away and shooting at what appeared to be the very tip of the mountain. This is more or less how you shoot a rifle; you look right down the top of the barrel at the target and fire, except in this case it was a very big rifle.

I walked over to the young gunners on the gun and asked them what they were doing. They looked up and were a little surprised to see a colonel just walk over like that. So they said that they were firing against what they thought was a sniper position on the side of that hill. I said, "That's great. You mind if I shoot some?" Well, they looked at each other a little puzzled and said, "Sure, sir. Come on!" So I got in there, put a couple rounds in the howitzer, pulled the lanyard back and fired a couple of 105 rounds for the cause of freedom. That was pretty exciting for me. I think they got a kick out of it, too. When I got back to my HQ I sent a note to a couple of my old Artillery buddies telling them what I was doing in Afghanistan. Who'd have guessed it?

Another form of fire support that we have are mortars. The U.S. Army basically has three sizes of mortars: a small 60mm mortar, a medium-sized 81mm mortar, and then a larger 4.2-inch mortar. Mortars, of course, fire high-angle rounds, relatively short distances, maybe 5 or 6 kilometers depending on the type of weapon system. Plus, they're mobile so we can move them around fairly quickly.

I'll never forget the meeting we had one night at a camp in Asadabad. Before we went to bed the leadership got together and talked about the plans for the next day — some patrols that were ongoing, some work that we were doing with the locals. Just before we walked back to our tents the detachment commander said, "Remember, we're going to fire the mortars tonight. At about 0200, we're going to fire some illumination rounds up along the ridge just to let the enemy know that we're here and we can reach out and touch them if need be." That is called H & I fire, harassment and interdiction fire.

It just so happened that my tent was right next to the 81mm gun pit. I went back there after the meeting at the end of a long, hard day and dropped off my stuff under my cot and got ready to go to bed. My RTO, my radio operator, who traveled with me, was in the cot next to mine. So we got in our beds and went to sleep.

Of course I was tired and I forgot to tell him about the H & I fire at 0200 that morning. Lo and behold, a few hours later there was a huge explosion right next to the tent. We both jumped up, grabbed our gear, put on our helmets, put on our flak vests and just as we were getting ready to run outside the tent, I looked at him and said, "Oh, yeah. Sorry, I forgot to tell you. Outbound mortar rounds at 0200." I looked at my watch and there it was right at 2:00 A.M. He looked at me with something like surprise and disgust and said, "I can't believe you forgot to tell me that. I thought they were incoming!"

They both sound the same when you are sound asleep at 0200 hours.

22

UW Thinking in a "Joint" Environment

The day after the attack at the new Lware A-camp, a man brought his child up to our camp, from the small village to our west. The child was six or eight years old and had been shot through and through, in one side and out of the other side of the shoulder. The village was to the west; we were shooting to the east. The bad guys were shooting to the west, over us and into this child's shoulder. So the father brought the child in and said, "This is what you Americans did." And we said, "No, no. We were shooting this way and they were shooting that way and you were behind us." And he said through our interpreters, "Okay. That makes sense. I understand."

We said, "Let us help you take care of this child." We had two SF medics. Their knowledge and their aid bags, pretty rudimentary by Western standards, took the Lware Province a thousand years into the future from their medieval medical practices. So we said, "Let us help you take care of the child. If we can't do it here, we'll fly you and the child to a hospital. We can sew him up here or do surgery at the hospital if needed. We'll take special care with your child."

"No," he replied. "Not going to do it. I will walk to Pakistan." At the beginning of our efforts in Lware, the locals were still fearful of the Afghan government presence as well as that of the U.S. Army. So fearful that a father would turn down medical care for a child and walk through the mountains to Pakistan rather than receive aid from us.

Those were the kinds of attitudes in the province when we first occupied and stood up the Lware A camp. The locals distrusted us to such an extent that a father with a seriously wounded child would rather walk five miles than take a helicopter ride back to an American hospital.

Fast forward three or four months more to the summer of 2004. The people of Lware Province voted in the first-ever presidential election. And they felt confident enough in their security to vote in President Karzai. Before the A-team moved into the region with their Afghan forces, it was basically against the law to be a woman in public. Now women made up 40 percent of the voters. Astonishing! It was amazing that nearly half the voters were women in an area that had been an Al-Qaeda sanctuary just a few months prior. Again we accomplished this by operating *by, with and through* the Afghans. We set up an Afghan border checkpoint with an Afghan flag, Afghan border police, and Afghan soldiers. We replicated this at about fifteen locations, fifteen other A-camps across Afghanistan, predominantly up and down the Afghan-Pakistan border. These were Special Forces A-camps, not American "fire bases." We did not simply project *fire* power. We came in like Tom Sawyer; we projected *unconventional warfare* power.

Lware was probably one of the best examples of how UW can provide the results we are looking for in this war on terror. This Lware camp's tactical success was facilitated by about fifteen or so American UW experts, not by an army of men swarming over the hills. The "face" of that camp was Afghan. This Special Forces A-team that was there for the duration of my command consisted of a dozen men, a small civil affairs team, and a small psychological operations team, each one with about three or four Americans. The main force consisted of two or three hundred Afghan soldiers and the camp was truly *their* camp. Now *this* was a tactical success.

The challenge for me was that tactical success had to be carried over to the strategic level. How could we turn the entire war into one where we helped the locals carry the banner? How could we universally facilitate the indigenous capabilities to conduct all missions, whether building roads, building schools, gathering information, or conducting raids or ambushes? You value something you earn more than something you're given. When you paint it yourself, you're proud of your white picket fences—and you want them to stay that way. *By, with, and through!*

The authorizing commander for any direct action raids was the

Joint Task Commander. He was my immediate boss. His HQ was across the street from my CJSOTF compound at the old Soviet air base at Bagram Airfield. I commanded the CJSOTF, Combined Joint Special Operations Task Force.

I was assigned to the JTF, and I had two different JTFs while I was there. For the first 8 months or so of my Afghan tour, we worked for JTF18, which was built up around the 10th Mountain Division. They were part of the Army's 18th Airborne Corps, thus the number JTF 18. The 10th MD, thus the JTF commander, was MG Lloyd Austin.

His command rotated home to their base at Ft. Drum, New York, and was replaced by the 25th ID out of Schofield Barracks, Hawaii, under the command of MG Eric Olson. They renumbered the JTF to JTF 76, for our year of independence, 1776.

Each of those divisions brought their own headquarters and most of their combat formations, an aviation brigade, one or two infantry or artillery brigades, and their division support brigade. Then, once in theater, they were augmented by units like mine, Special Operations, additional international forces, Air force and Marine units. These augmentations doubled or tripled their size from an infantry division to a Joint Task Force.

It is similarly true for a Special Forces Group. I commanded the 3rd Special Forces Group (forward) in Afghanistan. We were augmented with an SF battalion from the Army National Guard, two companies from the Army Reserves, a couple of USMC companies for local security at one of the A-camps, a platoon of SEALs, several individual staff officers, and, of course, battalion-size forces from several other nations. Most of us met for the first time in Afghanistan. Needless to say, we had a steep learning curve.

My CJSOTF added up to about 4,000 men and women from 6 nations, including all the U.S. military services and each active and reserve component. We all got along very well, because we were focused on a singular mission. While we may have showed up with different ideas of success, I tried hard and I tried early to get the ideas in sync with a common mission and vision.

My theme was simple, because with that many people from that many backgrounds, simplicity is the best answer. "No matter what the question, the first answer is to get the locals to do it." That was our mission, that was our theme, that is what we all tried to do.

The SEAL platoon commander with me in Afghanistan was a friend, Commander Chuck Wolf, with whom I had taken a course at Harvard University some years ago. We were both sent to Harvard for a course in International Conflict Management at the Kennedy School, with several high-ranking foreign officers. The Navy Special Operations Command sent one field grade officer, Chuck. And the Army Special Operations Command sent one field grade officer, me. It was part of the various Department of State initiatives to build friends among third-world military leaders. But by coincidence, he was the SEAL commander in Afghanistan and is a great guy and I thought a lot of him. Special Operations is a small community, even between the services.

My Joint Operations Center (JOC) had multiple computers and representatives from all the commands and all across my staff. I had a personnel expert, intelligence expert, operations folks, logistics, I had the weather guy, the air planners. I had liaisons from each of the commands. I had secure radio and telephone communication to all the commands. Most systems were secure to the secret level, but I had a couple of phone lines rated at the Top Secret level, too. We had communication to higher and adjacent HQs as well and I could call them when needed. Any of those sections had a watch officer sitting in the JOC 24/7. The Joint 2 was the Intel section, for example, with a J2 section working in a tent away from my JOC, but they had a J2 desk at the JOC. So I could come to the JOC and say, "What's the status of Jalani? Where do we think he is and when's the last time somebody had eyes on him?" And the guy either had the answer or he had his search engine, figuratively, back in their J2 section that could track it and get the reports.

If we had UAV overhead, which we did several times, really for specific preplanned targets or operations, we could get basically a black and white real-time video, kind of grainy but good enough to see somebody running across a field, good enough to see gunshots and explosions behind them as we chase them across the field.

We'd put the drone video on a big screen. In case the unit in contact needed some support, we'd know enough about the situation to try to have it ready before they asked. The term "in contact" means in contact with the enemy, in a firefight.

A good JOC battle captain knows the questions before they are asked. I was blessed with several great battle captains. Most of them were senior Special Forces captains who had just given up command of an A-team and were about to be promoted to major. Questions covered the span of staff responsibilities. What's the status of our replacements for First Battalion? First Battalion's going home next month: are the new soldiers here yet? When are they coming in and when are the outgoing soldiers leaving? One company comes in this week and the other leaves the following week; do we have enough billeting for them all or do we need to put up some temporary shelters?

I had a pretty detailed financial office as well, because I used three or four different authorities to spend money. I frequently got budget updates. Here's how much money we have in each account, here's what we spent it on. Are we above the power curve or below it? If we continue to spend the same amount of money each month on arming the local militias, will we go broke early or can we continue past the spring?

A glide path is really just a budget plan. We're scheduled to spend this much money every month and I need to know if we're above that amount or below it. Depending on the source of the money, that would give me different authorities. Some money I could use only for intel collection, other funds for extra security efforts for my soldiers living out in the hinterlands.

My only real restriction on my intelligence funds was that we could not buy drugs or prostitution to co-opt a source. But my intel experts could buy them anything else. My thinking was that we could not "buy" their loyalty forever, but we could rent it for a while. And that is a good start.

My budget officer was an Army finance officer with finance insignia. She was an elementary school teacher who signed up for a tour in the active Army right after 9/11 and found her way to managing and tracking some of the most complex accounting in the world. America is blessed with an abundance of talent and passion. As an added benefit, she had a marvelous voice and used it to sing several times in our small chapel. Hearing "Amazing Grace" spill from an old Soviet barracks across the Afghan plain is a wondrous sound.

23

Czech Republic Paratroopers

Czechoslovakia, a former Soviet satellite, had split into two countries, Slovakia and the Czech Republic. One of the six nations that had a force under my command was the Czech Republic. They deployed to Afghanistan shortly after I got there, the first Czech force ever to be deployed out of their country for military operations.

At that point they were just preparing to join NATO. Their joining NATO would be the final separation in their relations with the old Soviet Union, and it was clear to me, in the first ten minutes after I met with these Czech soldiers, that they were ready for NATO. Every single one — smart, articulate, athletic — was ready to get after the terrorists and prove themselves to the world. They were proud to be there and they were going to make a difference while they were there. Obviously, I enjoyed working with them very much.

One of the keys to being a good coalition force commander is using these different nationalist forces in ways that best complement their respective attributes vis-à-vis the mission — again, to use the right golf club in your bag at the right time and in the right way. So what the Czechs brought with them were well-trained soldiers who were well armed, that had a sophisticated, secure communications node set up, and who could go out in small teams and conduct reconnaissance deep into Taliban areas, both zone and point reconnaissance, strategic reconnaissance.

They also had the capability for short, violent, direct-action missions if we ever got enough target information to plan such a mission. What I used the Czech soldiers for was to do just that, to infiltrate into

Taliban areas and conduct a series of zone reconnaissance operations, to check out areas, to look for people, to look for signs of Al-Qaeda and Taliban, to get to know the ins and outs of an area. And also to conduct what we called strategic reconnaissance, which is to place very small teams on hilltops and look up and down valleys to observe operations of the enemy, to observe activities, and, if the opportunity presented itself, to call in fire missions either from U.S. Air Force jets overhead or from traditional tube artillery units if they were within the fairly limited range of the guns.

These Czechs did an awesome job with these reconnaissance missions. Never once did they get into a situation that they couldn't handle.

One time in particular they were on a reconnaissance mission up in the northeast of the country not too far from one of my A-camps in Asadabad. They were in a very rough region. These Czech soldiers observed, as it turned out, another NATO force from a great distance and had the wherewithal to think about what they were doing, get on the radio, make a series of radio calls, and ultimately realize that these were friendly forces coming towards them.

The immediate reaction in a situation like that is to shoot first and ask questions later. Only a disciplined professional force could have acted as they did on that cold dark mountain. That is the most high-risk operation on the battlefield, when two friendly forces accidentally bump into each another, because either force can inflict casualties on the other. But these Czechs were able to get out of that situation nicely.

One day, at my headquarters at Bagram Air Base about an hour north of Kabul, Afghanistan, one of my subordinate commanders was briefing us on his plan for a pending area reconnaissance mission. Included in this briefing were my boss, Maj. Gen. Lloyd Austin, who was the Joint Task Force commander (JTF) at the time, and also included the commander of a battalion of men from the Czech Republic who were fighting with us in Afghanistan.

It just so happened that the Czech commander, MG Austin, and I were walking out of the briefing at the same time, and as we crossed the small parking lot I turned to Gen. Austin and said, "Sir, did you know that you're standing between the only two Czech Army paratroopers in

Central Asia that are colonels?" The Czech commander was both a colonel and a paratrooper; of course; it just so happened that I was the other. General Austin looked at me and asked the obvious question, "Really? How did that come about?"

During the Cold War, every soldier in our military had an emergency war plan mission. When I was an A-team commander, a captain, years ago in 3rd Battalion, Tenth Special Forces Group, my ODA's mission, my A-team's mission, was to parachute into Czechoslovakia, using one of several large lakes as our drop zone, swim to shore and blow up a series of bridges and dams that would slow or stop the Russian assault that we anticipated across Czechoslovakia. The strategic goal was to stop the second and third echelon reinforcements from the invading Soviet force that we anticipated would come across Europe. After our initial direct actions missions of destroying bridges and dams, my ODA and I were to link up with Czech partisans and fight against the Soviets using unconventional warfare tactics — in short, leading a guerrilla war against the communists.

But after the breakup of the Soviet Union, as a company commander in 3rd Battalion, Tenth Special Forces Group — I commanded Alpha Company, which had the company headquarters and 6 ODAs in it. We received a mission to conduct the first Partnership for Peace program between American Special Forces and the new Czech Republic. My mission was to set up some joint training exercises between the American Special Forces and the Czech Republic Airborne Regiment.

I went over there for a few weeks with a very small team for this first interaction. As a young Green Beret major, I took another SF officer from the battalion operations section and a sergeant from the battalion HQ. I also took a former officer in that old army, in the Czechoslovakian army, the Soviet puppet army. He was born in Prague, went to school in Prague, and was a lieutenant in the Czechoslovakian army for a couple of years. He ultimately escaped to the West through Germany. He went skiing one day, but instead of skiing down the left side of the mountain back into Czechoslovakia, he skied down the right side of the mountain and kept on going all the way to Germany.

He made his way to the United States and ultimately enlisted in the United States Army. He then joined the Special Forces regiment and went with me back to his home country to act as my interpreter and, of course, to help me learn about the country. He was a great asset but, what's more, a fine soldier. For me, soldiers like him made a quarter of a century of military service go by in a flash.

One day as we walked down one of the streets in Prague, he pointed at a modest building and said, "That's my parents' house right over there."

"Do they even know you're here?" I asked with astonishment.

"No, they don't," he responded.

"You need to go see them," I said, "let them know you're here and alive." In short, the soldier and his family had a great reunion. What a wonderful story.

We linked up with the Czech paratroopers to learn from them and also to teach them what we knew about running an army in a democratically elected society. *Running an army in a democratically elected society* was a fairly new concept to them. So we trained each other in classes and discussions, but we also conducted a joint airborne operation. That meant that my soldiers and I would jump with a Czech parachute out of a Czech MI-8 helicopter. The MI-8 is an old Soviet troop transport and utility helicopter. We planned and briefed the operation on one day and got ready to do it the next day. The night before our jump day, the Czech paras invited us out to a local pub near their base in the Czech Republic to have a drink. Of course, we knew this was coming.

I absolutely loved the idea of getting out there with them and getting a flavor of their homeland and culture, but I long ago learned never try to drink with a Central European, because they've been drinking vodka since they were babies. So I told my two guys that we would have a couple drinks only and then say farewell. So we did.

We had the appropriate shot of vodka with all the other paras (paratroopers), chased it with a good glass of Czech beer, and chatted as best we could at the bar. Several of the Czechs were very excited to talk to an American and gladly spoke with me in English. They said they knew all about our country because they'd seen the TV show *Dallas*. They assumed that I lived in a place like South Fork, something I often heard when I was overseas.

As we got to know them a little bit, I looked around and said, "Now what kind of incentives do you offer your soldiers to encourage them to re-enlist? You get them in the army, you train them to become soldiers, then you train them to become elite paratroopers. They're excellent soldiers. What do you have for them to motivate them to re-enlist?"

He looked at me like he'd never heard such a question before. "Re-enlist?" he asked. "Why on earth would they re-enlist? Nobody re-enlists in the Czech army. They come in, do their two years of compulsory service, and then they go home."

"Well, how many sergeants do you have in this battalion?" I responded.

"We have two sergeants," he said. "The battalion is run by lieutenants and, of course, more senior officers, and the staff at headquarters is manned by privates."

Essentially, he was telling me they had a battalion full of privates with less than two years, a few lieutenants right out of college as squad leaders, a few platoon leaders, and then the commander and his staff. An interesting concept, an army of privates, which was very Soviet-like, but the battalion was, nonetheless, a good organization.

Going home after just a couple of drinks turned out to be a *great* call on my part. The next morning we got to the drop zone, the helicopter landed, the paratroopers were lined up, we'd been given our CZ parachutes and put them on, and we were ready to go. We'd had the jumpmaster personal inspection (JMPI) on our Czech parachutes to make sure they were on properly. I gave my two American troopers another JMPI just to make sure everything important looked to be hooked up and serviceable. We all knew what to do.

Now, I don't think this old helo, which had hydraulic fluid and oil dripping or oozing from every single possible location, had been maintained in the previous 10 or so years. We climbed on anyway, and I noticed that the pilots were not wearing uniforms, but matching jogging suits. I was amazed. You would never see an American pilot do that.

We sat down in our jump seats, looked across at the jumpmaster, and realized he was the ringleader from the vodka drinking contest the night before. He looked like he was just one very small step away from the grave, both eyes red, just barely moving.

When it came time to jump out of that airplane, he looked me in the eye — with only one eye because he could only open one — reached over with his left hand, slid the helicopter door open, pointed at me, and then pointed his thumb out the door as if to say, "You go." Then he closed his working eye and laid his head back against the side of the aircraft.

In short, this was a sharp contrast to our experience. When an American jumpmaster gives commands to go, they are very deliberate. There is no doubt in anyone's mind that the jumpmaster is in charge. You have been deliberately inspected. You get warnings at 6 minutes, 2 minutes, 30 seconds, 15 seconds, standby, and then "go" when it is time to jump out of the door.

I looked at that hung-over Czech para and then looked at my two guys and said, "Well, gents, I guess that's us. Let's go." Off we went. Not to worry, you can bet that before we left the aircraft I'd made sure we were safe. The three Americans were experienced paratroopers, our gear was on properly, and we were ready.

We jumped with them three times that day and wound up having a great time. Their parachutes were static line parachutes, very similar to ours, with a chest-mounted release as opposed to a waist-mounted release that we use on American parachutes. I had used a chest-mounted release when I first started jumping out of airplanes some twenty-five years ago. Despite their seemingly unorthodox approach, their gear was certainly in order.

We did, in fact, hit the ground after every jump, and more importantly, got up after we hit the ground after several jumps that day.

When I left Afghanistan, the Czechs paid me a great compliment. I was awarded the Czech Republic Distinguished Service Cross. I'm fairly certain I am the only American who is both a Czech paratrooper and recipient of that award, and I am very honored to wear them both on my uniform, even to this day.

After my change of command ceremony, and just a day before I left Afghanistan for home, I conducted the first interview that I did from Afghanistan — and I did that on a Czech radio station. I was honest and complimentary: these Czech soldiers under my command were great soldiers. I chose them for the first interview because of the timing (right before I went home) and the locations. I figured that the enemy was less likely to listen to Czeck radio than he was to follow the American press.

24

The Press

When I tell people that I did that radio station interview, I sometimes get puzzled looks. I know what they're thinking before they say it — a Special Forces commander has some of the darkest of the dark ops people under his command: what's Colonel Herd doing in the press?

I believe that information is a weapons system. Most people don't think of it that way, but we do. On the one hand, information lets us talk to our supporters and reward their faith in us by showing them exactly what we're doing, but it also lets us talk to our *enemies* and possibly influence them. I'm not talking about propaganda. In most cases, the truth is actually a good news story. You aren't tempted to stretch the truth: you just turn on the lights and let folks see it. Sometimes it can disarm an enemy as surely as a bullet.

When I was first commissioned-in the early 1980's, the common thinking was that the press was the enemy. Don't talk to them, don't sit with them, don't share anything with them. Nothing good can come of it and worse, it might even hurt your chances of mission success.

As I matured, I realized that in most cases, that thinking was wrong. Knowing that the press was going to write *something*, I realized that I might as well help them write the right thing. As I said: in this war, information is a weapon system just as surely as if it were a bullet or a bomb, but it can be a lot more effective than a bullet or a bomb if it affects the way the enemy thinks, if it affects their willingness to fight. To paraphrase Sun Tzu, to defeat an enemy in battle is good, but to cause him not to fight at all is even better. We don't always have to reduce the enemy's *ability* to wage war; with smart information operations, we may be able to simply reduce the enemy's *willingness* to wage war.

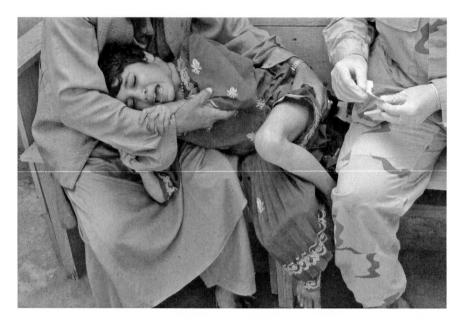

Our aid stations were of great value to the locals, as well as to our intel collection efforts. One of the gauges we had was the number of females that visited our clinics. Here, a father brings his daughter in for a shot. We knew we were successful when we saw women of child-bearing years at an SF clinic. That seldom happened, though.

In this global unconventional war on terrorism, information can make all of the difference. With that in mind, I invited three members of the press to one of my A-Camps in Afghanistan. One was a crew from a radio station in Pakistan, one was the U.S. TV show *60 Minutes*, and the third was more or less from my enemy's primary information source, Al Jazeera.

The leadership at the Joint Task Force and at Ft. Bragg recommended against it. Too risky, they said. You have no control over what they will show, say, or write.

Well, as we say, *fortune favors the bold*. Our press day proved to be one of the smarter decisions I'd made. Not surprisingly, Al Jazeera did not show up. Too bad; they would have seen the true face of the war, the west helping the locals fight against an aggressive and ruthless Taliban. We did have the radio station from Pakistan send a reporter. That was great. I knew that I would be talking directly to the Pakistani people because radio is how Pakistanis get their news.

We also had one of the commentators from *60 Minutes*, Lara Logan, spend about a month with our teams. In the end, the Pakistani radio and *60 Minutes* did great pieces for their audiences, both key constituents of this command. They interviewed Afghan civilians as they left our aid stations, and it was the Afghans who said we were helping them, not just our saying that. The Afghans we were working by, with and through got to hear the way we really are, and that usually makes friends out of people who don't know us very well.

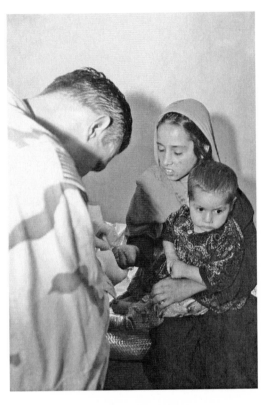

Here a girl of about 7 brings her younger sibling in for a visit to an SF clinic. The SF medics, with whatever they had in their aid bag and with the supplies we would eventually fly into a camp, would treat every possible ailment.

The other constituent was the American people. As I said, truth is usually a good news story, and the American people got to see us the way we were, too. From what I heard, the *60 Minutes* show went over well back home, which of course was a good thing. We want to reflect well on the country we love.

Just a day before I left Afghanistan for home, I was interviewed by a Czech TV station. It was the only interview from my Afghan tour in which I allowed my name to be mentioned. I made it a point during all of my other interviews when I was deployed never to allow my name to be mentioned on the radio, in newspapers, on TV or anything like that.

While I was happy to give interviews, I didn't want my name to be mentioned. This wasn't to be unfairly secretive. I think transparency is important. I just didn't want the enemy knowing the name of the current CJSOTF commander if I could help it. I saw no reason to make it easy for an angry Muslim extremist to Google my name and find my family just outside of Ft. Bragg.

My concern was not paranoia; it is a true understanding of the intent and the capability of our enemy. Terrorism is by nature unpredictable. I was there to fight terrorists and not add my family's name to a list of targets carried by some extremist.

Most of the media people that I worked with obliged my request and I was never quoted by name. Except for *U.S. News and World Report*.

I agreed to do an interview with three reporters simultaneously: one from *60 Minutes*, one from *USA Today*, and one from *U.S. News and World Report*. I told them all from the beginning, "I'm happy to talk to you. I want to talk to you about unconventional warfare and how we fight this war. But here's my request. Don't mention me by name because, quite frankly, if you say the *Special Forces commander Col. Walter Herd*, it's easy for the enemy then to track me down, track my family down to Fayetteville, right outside of Fort Bragg. I'm deployed for the duration, for a long duration. I don't want the Taliban to know where my kids go to school." Two of the three obliged. Against my very specific direction, the reporter from *U.S. News and World Report* mentioned me prominently and by name in his article. I was livid. For that infraction, he lost his credentials to conduct military interviews for the next year or so. Thankfully it didn't cause me or my family any harm.

But in most cases, I had come to respect the media and really appreciate their understanding of my situation. And after I returned home, I even wrote a couple of articles myself and gave several speeches about what our soldiers are doing over there and how to fight and win this war.

25

Fallen Comrades

Years ago, when I was a battalion commander, I woke up in the middle of the night, reciting the names and locations and dates of soldiers that I had commanded who had paid the ultimate price. It was a fairly short list at that time. Unfortunately, it's longer now. Some people have their "I-love-*me*" photos of themselves and some B-list celebrity in their office or home library. I have a plaque with the names of those soldiers with their regiments and the dates they were killed. And every year on the appropriate date, I raise a glass of Kentucky bourbon in their honor.

Whether the soldiers were killed in training or in combat is really irrelevant. They are heroes. Every one of them. Every soldier that's ever worn the uniform signed a blank check. Some of those checks are cashed in a big way and are paid for with their life. Some are cashed in a smaller way. Some aren't cashed at all. But everyone who signs that check and says, "Use me as needed," is a hero. I've enjoyed the company of good men and women: I've enjoyed the company of heroes.

For those soldiers in my command who died when I happened to be at home station, I would lead the death notification and I would try to do it in as kind and as loving a way as possible. The *death notification* is a no-notice personal trip to the soldier's widow. This is a *no fail mission*.

The first time I did it, I got a call early one Saturday morning that a soldier in my company had been killed in a parachute accident on a training exercise. I organized the company sergeant major, our battalion chaplain, and our family support group representative. Within about two hours, I went from my living room where I was peacefully reading the paper, to my office, and then to the new widow's front door.

My company sergeant major and my battalion chaplain and I did a quick rehearsal in the car on the way over there, before we knocked on her door. I told my sergeant major, Dave Farmer, a great American and a good friend, "Sergeant Major, I think I'm good for about two lines. I think I can say about two sentences before I am emotionally spent. I need you to come in right after I run out of words and you follow up. Chaplain, when he's finished, I need you to move in and offer some comfort." In any event, we wanted to be at her door before a single word of the accident had spread.

When she opened that door at about 11:00 on Saturday morning and saw three very somber faces in our dress uniforms standing on her front doorstep, she knew exactly why we were there. I saw the blood run out of this blessed woman's face. She turned white before I could say the first words.

After the three of us were there for about five minutes, our family support representatives, a couple of wives from the battalion, were coming around the corner.

The fact of the matter is, no matter who gives the new widow the terrible information, and no matter how well we do it, with as much love and compassion as we have, the person that knocks on the door is seen by the family as the *guilty party*, the one to blame.

What we try to do is notify the family, tell him or her absolutely everything we know, and then let their peers in the battalion offer more long-term support. But in my first notification, it was particularly hard. Even before I opened my mouth, I looked over the new widow's shoulder and saw a young girl, probably about three or four, watching television, watching the same cartoons that I knew my three-year-old daughter was watching back at our home. Needless to say, I choked back my own tears. By the grace of God, this woman's dearest friend was at the house having a cup of coffee and planning a day out with their kids. Now she was there to offer some support.

Fast forward almost exactly three years. When I was a battalion commander, a soldier of mine was killed in Kosovo. A lot of people think there were no U.S. combat deaths during our involvement in Kosovo, but there was one. One great American soldier, a staff sergeant we called "Super," because he was simply a super soldier, an American

Airborne Ranger Green Beret, was killed by a command-detonated ambush in the northern sector of Kosovo called Kosovo Kominiche.

Command-detonated means that there was an enemy soldier with his finger on the detonator when Super drove his Humvee over a mine and the enemy combatant squeezed the detonator, blowing up the Humvee, killing Super almost instantly and wounding his compatriot in the vehicle, who was from the same A-team.

I was in the United States when Super was killed in Kosovo. We did the same notification process. He was not married but he did have a girlfriend. I was preparing for the notification when the administrators of the program at the Ft. Carson personnel office called me and said, "Hey, listen. We only do notifications for family members. Don't go do the girlfriend. She can just get a phone call. You only have to do wives." I was adamant that we would notify the girlfriend with the same sense of compassion as a wife or parent. It was the right thing to do. So I went through the same process with her.

I tell you now, having done this a couple of times, I'd rather do almost anything than do another death notification. Bar none, this is the hardest thing I've ever done, but the day we fail to feel a family's pain is the day we cease to be human.

For a thousand years, militaries have tried to mask emotion by ceremony. That's why we have 21-gun salutes at funerals, so we can focus on the guns and not the deaths. No matter how much ceremony, how much rehearsal, no matter how shiny your brass is on your uniform, you do a death notification like these and it cuts straight to your heart.

With the soldiers I lost in Afghanistan, I was of course unable to knock on the door and talk to their families, but I wrote a letter to each one of them. That was equally painful.

One of the things I did in Afghanistan is what I call battlefield familiarization tours. I spent a lot of time traveling around the battlefield, talking to soldiers, seeing the land, seeing the people, making estimates, making sure my intent was being followed through. About mid–May of 2004, I went to one of my A-camps and spent a night or two there with my command sergeant major and my radio operator.

I talked to the ODA commander, Captain Dan Eggers, a smart young man who had just gotten there a couple of months before. He clearly got this thing called *unconventional warfare.* He took to it like a fish to water. When I was talking to him about my intent, he knew it better than I did. He understood that the default answer to every question is to *get the Afghans to do it.* The day that I first met Captain Eggers, he had just met with some of the local leaders and spoken with them in partial Arabic about what we could do to help them fight the Taliban — let me repeat, what we could do to help *them* fight the Taliban. This is the kind of stellar young officers we have in Special Forces.

Tragically, about two or three days after I met him, Captain Eggers and his team were on patrol in an area of potential enemy activity and were killed in a command-detonated ambush. In this particular case, the enemy's weapon systems were pretty rudimentary, even crude, yet very effective. The enemy had taken several pounds of explosives out of an old Soviet 120-mm rocket warhead. They'd buried them in the ground. They had wires going from these explosives through a fluorescent light switch like any light switch you would see on any wall. The light switch was hooked up to a car battery so that when they flicked the switch, the electricity would go into the old Soviet explosives and cause the explosion. That is exactly what happened when it blew up on May 29, Memorial Day weekend, and killed four great Americans on this team, one of them Capt. Dan Eggers.

I was in my headquarters at Bagram when we got that call over our secure satellite radios. My JOC, Joint Operations Center, began to work MEDEVAC coordination, anything we could do to help. I got on the phone to the battalion commander, a proud Tennessean, who was located at Kandahar several hours south of my headquarters. He stands about six foot four and gets your attention right away. He commanded the 2nd Battalion, 3rd Special Forces Group under the CJSOTF.

After he described the situation — who did what and what happened during the attack — before I could even say anything, he started to describe the counterattack that he had planned. He and his great soldiers did in fact conduct a counterattack. I think they killed about a dozen of those bastards who were responsible for the death of Dan Eggers and his men. I will say, though, had we killed a million of them, it's still not worth one drop of American blood. The Americans that we have in this global war on terror are not dying to kill the enemy. They are dying to maintain our freedom.

26

Quarters

People ask about our life in the military and one of the first things that comes to mind is our housing. In Afghanistan, I lived in a large tent with my command sergeant major. We both had a desk and a conference table for us to have small meetings with the key staff and commanders. About halfway through my tour, my tent was upgraded to a plywood "C Hut." I thought I had moved into Beverly Hills.

Back in America, some forts have nicer housing than others. When I was a colonel at Ft. Knox they had beautiful old brick homes built in the twenties for colonels. We loved it. Living there was like living in Mayberry.

In the two years we lived on post at Knox, we almost never locked our doors. No need to. Our kids played with the other colonels kids on the street. They rode their bikes to the elementary school across the soccer field in our back yard.

At Ft. Carson there were much smaller, aluminum-sided homes built in the sixties. We loved living there as well. The neighbors, their kids and the views, all great. From our front door, we had an uninterrupted view of the snow-covered Rocky Mountains. Also from our door, we looked across green meadows, right up to the top. I joked by saying we had a $50,000 house on a million-dollar lot.

Ft. Bragg has beautiful homes as well, although when we moved there after I attended the Army War College in Carlisle, Pennsylvania, the housing office said it would be a six-year wait to get housing on Ft. Bragg. "Six years!" I said with astonishment. "I'll be out of the Army in six years." So we ended up buying a house in downtown Fayetteville.

About six months after we moved into our new house, we got a call from the housing office saying that quarters were now available. Typically older forts have a small number of really nice old pre–World War II homes and then an additional number of more modern, yet not as nice, homes.

The Army changed the housing regulations in the 1950s or 1960s. Prior to World War II I think a colonel was authorized about 2500 feet in his quarters. A colonel in the prewar Army was a rare thing. Remember, Dwight Eisenhower was only a colonel prior to the war. Later, a colonel's authorization was changed to about 1600 feet. So depending on when the home was built, that's the size quarters the colonel lives in. Not all homes on Colonel's Row are the same.

At some of the big posts, particularly around MDW, Military District of Washington, there is general officer housing for the chief, the chief of staff of the army, and the chairman of the joint chiefs, and those homes obviously are very nice. But again, it depends on the era in which the homes were built. The colonel's house I lived in at Ft. Knox was nicer than the commanding general's house down the street from ours at Ft. Carson. The quarters are numbered. Quarters One on every base is the commanding general's house. If you go back to some of these forts, like Ft. Benning, and look at Quarters One, you'll see Omar Bradley's name and some of the great heroes of our country who lived there. The one major exception to that rule is Ft. Myers in Washington, D.C. At Ft. Myers, Quarters One is for the Chief of Staff of the Army.

Usually the tradition and history of a unit is kept within that unit. The major unit in a fort will sometimes have a museum, or their headquarters building will display all the heraldry of the flags and war trophies. For example, the 82nd Airborne at Ft. Bragg, North Carolina, has a huge museum which displays all their regalia from multiple wars. It is beyond impressive.

In Special Operations, Special Forces is fairly new — 50 years old — therefore we don't have colors and weapons dating back to Gettysburg. And a lot of what Special Forces has accomplished under the radar screen, so there's not a lot of pomp and circumstance. I am proud to say that my flag, called the "colors," from Afghanistan now rests in the small Special Forces museum at Ft Bragg.

27

Winning in Afghanistan: Understanding the Culture

If you go back to force reciprocity and look at it from an unconventional warfare perspective, you start to see the new math needed for the road that we so rarely take. As my politically incorrect, but brutally honest, soldiers quickly realized: if the Taliban were disciplined Europeans, a lot more of us would be dead. But thank God, "Taliban don't aim," as they say. They simply can't shoot. They share the trait of poor marksmanship. It's the mindset of "if Allah wants the bullet to hit, then it'll hit so I don't need to waste my time aiming." European culture is different. They think God gave them eyes so they can aim and hands so they can hold steady. Not the Afghans. That is why we can be happy the Taliban are not Europeans.

When the Soviets left Afghanistan in 1989 they left the Afghan people's army with divisions, brigades, tanks, helicopters, jet fighters, and all the equipment needed for modern war. When the Soviets left, everything was running and in near perfect order. But if you don't do maintenance on mechanical things, they just stop running. The mindset of Afghans is that of about a 1000 B.C. culture. To check the hydraulics on the rotor lift of a helicopter is not inherent to their culture. In a largely illiterate society, something like that just isn't a norm.

The theory of relativity applies in societies. You don't have to be a first-world country; you just have to be better than the guys in front of you. In Afghanistan, the guys you are fighting are individuals with AK-47s, not divisions or corps of mechanized warriors. You don't need F-15s and tank brigades to win. You have to be a decent platoon leader who can do platoon maneuvers, make a few radio calls, and use big machine guns. And that's it. You're light years ahead. The road not taken is to focus on the indigenous capabilities. The road taken was to conduct a large-scale-maneuver American war. That was the wrong road.

About once or twice a week during my tour as the Combined Joint Special Operations Task Force commander in Afghanistan, I had dinner or tea with various Afghans, all the way from warlords to village elders to neighbors and friends of the soldiers in my Special Forces A-camps. I had tea with President Hamid Karzai on two occasions.

I remember the first time I went to the presidential palace, I was met at the massive front doors by his personal security detail. They were all Americans in their 20s or 30s, well armed and dressed in casual field gear, like what you'd find in an REI or L.L. Bean mail order catalog. I expect they were security contractors, probably former soldiers, but not current soldiers.

One of them asked me to give him all of my weapons before I could go into Karzai's office. Having been armed 24/7 since I got into Afghanistan, I hesitated.

He looked at me and said, "I know, Colonel, but the last several leaders of this country have been killed in that room. Karzai is determined not to be the next. I'll give them back to you when you leave."

We looked at each other and those unsaid words that go between soldiers were clear: No one wants to be disarmed. I carry weapons, I sleep with weapons—but I had no choice but to disarm. That's an unnatural thing for a soldier to do, but that was what this mission needed.

I handed over my pistol, my rifle, my knives and ammunition and walked into the room. I felt naked.

Of course, every culture has different etiquette rules while eating dinner. Needless to say, the etiquette for eating in Afghanistan was much different from what I learned growing up in Kentucky, at private schools and going to cotillion. I'll never forget my first meal with an Afghan village elder and his family (only the men) and a couple of my soldiers.

Now remember, in the Islamic world, the left hand is the *unclean* hand. You never eat with it and you never touch anybody with it. Of course, at most of these meals they used no eating utensils. What I noticed that most of the Afghan men did was either put their left hands behind their backs or in their pockets, and eat with their right hands. Therefore I did the same.

Another norm in the Muslim world is that showing the soles of your shoes or feet to someone is an insult — almost like giving someone "the finger" in our country. So when there are no chairs, which is normally the case when eating out in the hinterlands of Afghanistan, you basically squat down on your knees and sit on your ankles. That's not an easy feat for most Westerners, particularly old paratroopers with arthritic knees, but nonetheless I managed to sit through and enjoy countless dinners with Afghan men.

A couple of things to note: I never had dinner with an Afghan woman. In fact, I never even saw an Afghan woman of child-bearing years. The only Afghan females I saw were small children or old women. Any culture that arbitrarily writes off half of their intellectual capital has limited their potential for progress.

When I went into this village, one of the first I visited, I realized I was living in the Old Testament. I expected Moses to walk around the corner at any time. We are speaking here, through an interpreter, to one of the village elders about their relations with the Taliban and any foreigners.

Second thing: Afghans typically eat off a common plate. A table-cloth or a blanket is set out on the ground and a large plate, maybe two feet in diameter piled with rice, goat meat, chicken, and a couple of vegetables, is placed in the middle. A soft bread and bottled water or Pepsi or Seven-Up completes the setting. I always thought that soda was interesting and so out of place, but there it was.

Once the plate was set, we Westerners and the Afghans would sit around the blanket, squat down on our knees and reach over with our right hand into this common, large plate; pick up a mound of rice, and simply eat it out of our right hands. Sometimes we put it on the bread and made a bit of a sandwich.

The first time I participated in the ritual of taking a meal, I looked around at the Afghan mountains—eight or ten thousand feet; tall, rugged mountains; rugged men!

The Afghans had beards, of course, and so too did most of the American SF guys. When you shovel a handful of rice in your mouth and you've got a beard, you end up with rice all over your face. I couldn't help but think, "Man, what would my mother do if she could see me now?" I'm pretty sure nobody at the food preparation table washed his hands. Who knows where the food came from? But by the grace of God, with all those meals I was only sick once, which I considered a small miracle.

My meeting with the president was mixed. He wanted to talk about bringing the Taliban back into Afghan society. He supported the idea of their reentry if for no reason except to help them get jobs and to become less susceptible to entreaties from the radical arms. I concurred. Most of the rank and file Taliban are just poor folks with nothing better to do.

For some reason, he got no traction on the idea, probably because many of the U.S. conventional thinkers were more interested in killing Taliban than in converting them. Rather than killing all of the fish, I just wanted to change the temperature of the water so they could not survive as terrorists.

Now, if you think all meals are served with a common plate on a blanket out in the mountains, you'd be wrong. One night I was invited to dinner with an Afghan named Mardock. He went by General Mardock. He had a very nice, western-style home in Kabul, which is about an hour south of my headquarters at Bagram Air Base. Kabul, of course, is the national capital for the Afghan government. Bagram was an old Soviet air base. My headquarters was actually in an old Soviet motor pool building in Bagram. On Easter morning, we had a sunrise service on the roof of that old Communist maintenance bay. We enjoyed the irony of worshiping in a building built by communists. The overall joint task force (JTF) was headquartered across the street from me in the old Soviet control tower area.

That particular evening, I made up a convoy of three armed vehicles with drivers and armed escorts. Guns out, SA high. I took the British liaison officer to the joint task force with me. We drove from Bagram Air Base to Kabul, and when we arrived we left our drivers and security detail outside. The British liaison and I went inside to meet General Mardock. His home is very beautiful and has many western amenities. General Mardock also spoke excellent English, which was partially due to the fact that he went to the U.S. Army Armor Center as a student while he was fighting the Soviets in the seventies. He even had some of his children living in America at the time.

The meeting was incredible on a number of levels, and we spent three hours there. General Mardock had taken the opportunity of my visit to invite each of his former commanders to his house.

I met and talked with about fifteen or twenty Afghan Mushahdeen who currently lived on and had tribal relations up and down the Pakistan-Afghan border. One of them commanded a Mushahdeen force that brought down thirty Soviet helicopters during a three-day period during the Soviet-Afghan war. I asked him how he did it. "Pretty simple," he said.

The mountains in that country rise to peaks of about 24,000 feet. Helicopters, Soviet or American, can't fly over a mountain that high, so they're forced to fly down in the valleys. Well, after a while, the Mushahdeen would figure out the favorite routes that the Soviet pilots would take, and they would simply line those valleys with hundreds of Mushahdeen fighters firing RPG (rocket-propelled grenades) at the helicopters.

The RPG is a World War II–era piece of technology, not sophisticated, very simple. It's basically a hand grenade flying through the air. An inexperienced shooter can usually hit a target up to about a hundred meters or so. But if it hits a helicopter, it can do extreme damage. And in fact it did bring down about thirty helicopters in that three-day period against the Soviets.

Incidentally, the Taliban and Al-Qaeda use the same technique as the Mushahdeen did. Fortunately, they could not muster the numbers that the Mushahdeen could.

I remember the first helicopter flight I took in Afghanistan in a CH-47, a U.S. Army Chinook from the 10th Mountain Division. We were flying from one camp to the other at night. I was visiting a couple of my camps to see some soldiers and learn the lay of the land. I had my head out of the chopper's window, which is on the left side of the aircraft right behind the pilot, with the M-60 machine gun pointed out the window. I was looking out into the darkness, and just happened to turn my gaze down and saw an RPG being fired and coming our way. I'll never forget, it looked just like a sparkler that a kid plays with on the 4th of July being thrown at you in the dark. Sparks going kind of in a circle, not necessarily straight. Luckily we were high enough and fast enough so that by the time it got to our altitude we were long gone.

But that tactic would have worked well if fired in massive numbers. The Mushahdeen fired three or four hundred RPGs at helicopters that one weekend, almost three decades ago, to great effect.

Another one of General Mardock's Mushahadeen fighters had commanded an ambush against the Soviets that produced the highest number of casualties the Soviet Union had ever suffered in a single encounter since fighting the Nazis at Stalingrad.

Again, these high mountain peaks basically force the enemy to walk along the banks of a narrow canal, in this case, a narrow trail on the low ground. As the Soviets were going down one of their favorite routes, the Mushahdeen deployed hundreds of fighters up on the high ground and conducted an ambush. With RPGs, they killed the first vehicle and then the last vehicle and then went one by one killing some three hundred armored vehicles holding, probably, eight hundred Soviets. They wiped out every single one of them in what amounted to about a one-day battle.

We had dinner with General Mardock around a nice dining room table with china and sterling silverware. Beautiful home, beautiful dinner. Afterwards, General Mardock politely asked my British friend and me to join him in his living room on his couches. He asked us if we wanted a drink. Not only was the general the only Afghan man I met and spoke with who did not have a beard, he also was the only Afghan man I met and spoke with who, at least in my presence, smoked tobacco and drank alcohol, and I couldn't help but think I would *love* to have a drink.

I hadn't had a drink in almost a year, and about two days into my Afghan tour, I realized that if there was any place in the world that needed to relax and have a cold beer, it was here in Afghanistan. However, General Order Number One precludes American soldiers from drinking alcohol in Afghanistan. That order was put into effect to negate any insult to our Muslim hosts.

Two of only three or four discipline problems I had while commanding in Afghanistan were with soldiers breaking General Order Number One—which, incidentally, is a wonderful compliment to the 4,000 men and women in my command that after a year of war, I only had a small number of discipline issues. I expect the dean of students at any small college in America has more than that on a weekly basis.

"No thank you, sir," I replied accordingly. "I appreciate the offer." He offered me a cigarette. "Again, no thank you. I appreciate the offer. I don't smoke cigarettes." Then, perhaps to his surprise, I added, "I do, however, smoke a cigar. Would you mind if I light the one that I have with me?" So I enjoyed the only vice any of us could enjoy in Afghanistan—a really good Cuban cigar. And a can of Pepsi.

28

The UW Option

Then the general got down to business. "Colonel Herd, would you like help closing the border?" By that, of course, he meant the border between Afghanistan and Pakistan. He had my attention from that point on. My higher headquarters, Joint Task Force 180, had been working for months to figure out how to close that very porous, ambiguous and unmarked border. Everybody knew that Al-Qaeda and the Taliban had a safe haven inside the region of Waziristan on the Pakistani side of the border. So when a very pro-western Afghan leader asked me if I wanted to close the border, I realized I had just struck gold.

"Yes, sir, of course we'd love your help," I replied enthusiastically. "What are you thinking?"

While General Mardock was fighting the Russians, he commanded forces that lived on both sides of the border, a network of about two dozen military commanders that was still in place and that had tribes and family members on both sides of the border.

The border runs along what is called the "Durand Line." It's a 2,640-kilometer border that is poorly marked, ambiguous and without regard to tribal boundaries. It was established after the 1893 Durand Line Agreement between the government of colonial British India and Afghanistan and is named after Henry Mortimer Durand, who was the Foreign Secretary of British India at the time.

The commanders the general had invited to this meeting represented the very network he was offering to me — tested against the Soviets. Determined. Able to set up major operations. Those were the kind of combat leaders that General Mardock offered us in that simple question, "Would you like help closing the border?"

On the way home that night to Kabul, I began to realize that this could be the unconventional approach that we'd been looking for. This could be the way to focus *our war: by, with and through* the indigenous capability. When I got back to headquarters, I called my group plans officer, Lt. Col. Adrian Bogart, into my office. My office was a large Army tent with plywood floors and walls. On one end were two bunks, one for me and one for my command sergeant major. On the other side of the tent were our two desks and a large table.

Bogey is probably one of the smartest guys I've ever met. He's a strategic planner and Special Forces officer. I'd worked with him at the Pentagon five or six years prior and after not having seen him for some time, ran into him in an Army mess hall outside Baghdad about a year before my dinner with Mardock. I was over in Baghdad for a very short trip while I was assigned as the Chief of Operations for U.S. Army Special Operations Command at Ft. Bragg, a short assignment I was given before I took the command in Afghanistan. Bogey was just finishing an eight-month tour in Iraq. Highly, highly courageous soldier!

If you ask old Soldiers why they stayed in uniform so long, most of us will admit it is because we enjoy the company we were able to keep. Bogey's a perfect example. I fondly recall a meeting a couple of years after we got home, when he and his family joined me at my farm in Kentucky and we enjoyed a cool mint julep on our 200-year-old log cabin porch.

Now here we were in Iraq, negotiating very different terrain and meeting under very different circumstances. But, boy, was it great to see him! "Bogey, how you doing?" I greeted him in the Baghdad mess hall. "Long time, no see." Then, like any good soldier, I got down to business. "I'm taking over the CJSOTF in Afghanistan in a couple of months. Do you want to come with me?"

"Absolutely!" he replied, without hesitation.

I looked at him earnestly and said, "Bogey, think about that now. You've been over here for eight months. You sure you want to go to Afghanistan for another twelve?"

"Yes, sir," he again replied instantly. "Absolutely! I'd love to. Let me just talk to my wife first."

So he got his wife's blessing and two or three months later, after some time with his family and some much deserved R&R, he was back with me in Afghanistan.

Bogey and I sat around the map the next day after I'd met with Gen. Mardock and the Mushahdeen leaders and we drew small circles along the Afghan-Pakistan border. The circles represented the areas controlled by the Mushahdeen leaders that I had met.

So Bogey, my J3 director of operations, LTC Joel Woodward and I put together a plan called the Afghan National Guard, the ANG. Joel is another very smart guy and a brave, multi-combat tour Green Beret professional. The idea we came up with was to allow these regions to develop a National Guard force, much like we have in the United States where each state has a National Guard, such as the Kentucky National Guard, the Tennessee National Guard, the Florida National Guard, etc. And all the members of our national guards live predominantly in their respective states and train together, just like regular military. However, they could be called up to either work for the state in a natural emergency like a hurricane or tornado, or to work for the Federal government in a war or some other national need.

So the context for the Afghan National Guard (ANG) would be just that. The idea was that we'd support these Mushahdeen leaders to help them assess, recruit and train their own local National Guard force. These ANG forces would have American Special Forces advisors to train them, coordinate operations, and call in air strikes as needed. We'd make sure that all tactical units were in strategic synchronization. Then the national capital in Kabul could call them up into federal service and task them to secure their regions on the border, thus keeping the Taliban locked on one side or the other where they could be dealt with.

We put a lot of effort into the plan. We believed that for about five dollars a day we could get these soldiers to report for duty and become an army. We could form up several dozen battalions in almost no time because the Mushahdeen leaders already had their people standing by. That is one advantage to the high unemployment rate in Afghanistan: you can raise an army in a hurry.

They weren't standing by in uniform, of course. They were farming poppies or doing who knows what. But for about five dollars a day, we could bring these Afghan citizens to our side, take them off "sitting on the fence," speed up the economy, *and* close down the border. Since they were locals, they could gather local human intelligence, that

An Afghan Security Force soldier with an AK-47 (Kalashnikov) assault rifle in his hands, 7.62mm, and a PKM squad light machine gun at his feet, also 7.62mm. This soldier is one of the indig that was recruited, trained and organized by our forces, not as part of the Afghan National Army, but as part of our own UW force. They were great. Notice the decoration on his Kalashnikov. He "pimped" out the stock and grip, a very common practice among Afghan soldiers.

This Afghan is standing next to an old Soviet DSkH (pronounced "Diska") machine gun. The DSkH fires a round only slightly larger than the American M2 .50 caliber heavy machine gun. Therefore, in a pinch, the Russians could fire captured American .50 cal ammunition through their barrels, but we could not do the same with any captured Soviet DSkH ammunition. This is a good example of some strategic UW planning.

rare and valuable commodity that we had a really hard time getting as Westerners. And they could also get the locals to buy into the concept because the locals were their cousins, their in-laws, their nieces and nephews.

So I asked Lt. Colonel Bogart to put together our campaign plan so that we could comprehensively present it to higher headquarters for their approval and he obliged in a series of PowerPoint presentations and reports. I presented it to the Joint Task Force (JTF) 76 commander, Maj. Gen. Eric Olsen — who was also the commander of the 25th Infantry Division in Hawaii — shortly after he had taken over for MG Lloyd Austin.

The 25th Infantry Division arrived from Hawaii to Afghanistan during the second half of my tour to take command of the Joint Task Force from MG Austin and his 10th Mountain Division. When MG Olsen

After close inspection of both the weapons and the munitions, our SF weapons sergeants would help the indig "recycle" the captured gear. Here we fire a variant of the Soviet M60, 82mm recoilless rifle. These guns were designed for anti-tank warfare but are also useful as long-range direct fire systems in an UW effort.

first got to Afghanistan, I talked him through the concept of strategic unconventional warfare. He was very receptive.

One time, a month or two after he arrived, the Americans conducted a fairly large unilateral conventional combat operation in which they killed a large number of Taliban.

He asked me afterwards, "Walt, do you think we just killed a hundred Taliban or did we just create a hundred Taliban?" Clearly, that man understood unconventional warfare. MG Eric Olsen was very openminded, very supportive and, most importantly, very impressed with this Afghan National Guard concept.

I did have some limited means on my own authority to raise, assess, and train an indigenous force. We had some monies through U.S. Special Operations Command which were strictly for our own security and our own operations. So we used that authority and that funding to create a series of security forces among several of these A-camps.

Top: Additional firing shots from the recoilless rifle. *Above:* The SF weapons sergeant gives instruction on aiming and safety procedures of the newly captured weapon. "Safety procedures" are a foreign concept to the Afghan soldier.

This indig is wearing his recently purchased "tiger striped" uniform after his graduation from our basic training, run for the guard forces around our A-Camps. The best defense is a good offense, and this man is ready to run the ball down the field. He spent his entire life running up and down those mountains with his AK-47. Here, the SF A-Team is fighting *by, with and through* him.

We've no way of knowing if this cache of ammunition was saved for a rainy day, left over from the Soviet war, or intended for use by the Taliban. So we captured it, used what we could with our Afghan forces, and destroyed the rest. We used C4 demolition to destroy tons of munitions at a time.

One of the camps we had was in the Afghan city of Asadabad in the Konar province in the northeastern corner of the region. It was also where many of the U.S. combat forces were. We had a Special Forces company headquarters there called a B-team and two Special Forces A-teams along with some infantry soldiers, either Army or Marines, that moved in and out.

The company commander was Major Jeb Stuart. Major Stuart was a regular Army officer, a full-timer, a professional who commanded a National Guard company. I had put him in command of that company about a month or so earlier.

I had transferred the original company commander to a staff position at Bagram. The original commander brought the company over from the United States, and had fought with them for about four months,

Top: I pose for a glamour shot with a .50 cal DSkH heavy machine gun, one of many captured weapons after a successful raid we had with the Afghan soldiers in the lead. After weeks of gathering information through our indigenous intel network, we had enough clarity to unleash a company of Afghan soldiers with their SF advisors and capture these weapons from a local compound. *Above:* Another shot with Soviet 60mm mortars captured from a family "compound." While it is legal (and quite necessary) under Afghan law for men to carry individual weapons for their own protection, such crew-served weapons were out of bounds and therefore on our list to capture.

but he just wasn't getting the point of focusing on the fight *by, with and through*. I put Major Stuart in command and, within about three or four days, he absolutely had the picture. The world-class soldiers of that company, with his professional, unconventional leadership, took a quantum leap forward. And the picture that Jeb got was always to get the indigenous to conduct the operation. *By, with and through.*

I asked Major Stuart to raise his security force and conduct his UW mission, *by, with and through.* He did just that. When the day arrived to begin their training, there were several Afghan soldiers lined up. We told them to BYOG — that's *bring your own gun.* Luckily, at least in this instance, in Afghanistan every man has an AK-47. We'd provide uniforms and ammunition.

We showed the Afghan soldiers a couple of pictures from a mail order catalog, and let them pick the uniforms they liked. They selected some cool camouflaged uniforms and developed their own shoulder sleeve insignia of a scorpion superimposed on a triangle for their shoulder patch. It was easy to see they were highly motivated.

Jeb put the soldiers through an assessment phase — testing them physically and mentally — then a two-week basic training where they learned small arms, some basic tactics and some basic combat maneuver. Then Jeb and his SF soldiers began to advise these Afghan security forces on combat operations.

The first thing we had to do was gather intelligence. Again, these Afghan soldiers knew everybody in the neighborhood. They were related to everybody in the valley, so when we asked them, "Where are the Taliban?" and "Who supports Al-Qaeda?" one by one we began to track down bad guys. The Afghan security forces would conduct a raid, gather caches of munitions and demolitions, immediately conduct a human intelligence exploitation of the site, and interrogate in their own language *and* their own culture. This usually led to another operation which led to another operation and another operation.

This is how you fight an unconventional war. This is how you trigger long term change. Thirty or forty American soldiers, most of them Special Forces, directing action *by, with and through* the indigenous capabilities.

There's never been a prouder soldier than those new ASF I saw on

This Afghan proudly stands with his national colors. We made it a point to show their colors, not the U.S. colors, whenever we could. It is all about us helping them with their war and not their simply helping us in ours.

the day they graduated from their basic training and they began doing combat operations. It was a textbook example of unconventional warfare, right up there with what the SF team did in Lware.

So when you hear stories about the unconventional warfare success under Major Jeb Stuart in Asabadad and the UW success in places like Lware and dozens of others scattered across Afghanistan, you've got to ask yourself, "Why don't we do what we did at these Special Forces A-camps on a larger scale?" Well, the answer is frustrating and complicated.

29

The Challenge to
the UW Option

America has always had a fascination with special *operations* forces, SOF. Special Operations is an umbrella term for forces that have a broad spectrum of surgical combat capabilities. The special operations community contains truly elite soldiers, sailors, and airmen in their own right who conduct surgical, violent, unilateral U.S. combat operations. Nobody does unilateral surgical combat operations better than the Rangers and the SEALs, with U.S. Air Force and U.S. Army's 160th Special Operations Aviation Regiment support.

On the other hand, Special Forces soldiers are recruited and assessed and trained to conduct unconventional warfare, fighting the war *by, with and through* the indigenous people.

In 1986, Congress passed a law called the Nunn-Cohen Agreement. That law established the U.S. Special Operations Command as a four-star combatant command equal in stature to other commands like U.S. European Command and U.S. Central Command.

The law also stood up Army Special Forces as its own branch with its own career path and its own career progression. But it had an unfortunate twist. The Nunn-Cohen Agreement ultimately spelled out how many Special Forces units we would have, and how soldiers would be assessed and trained and selected as captains, majors, lieutenant colonels, and colonels. But when they get to the rank of general officer, the agreement says that Special Forces officers are moved out to a conventional combatant command or as a U.S. Code Title Ten force production officer.

Either way, in plain English, that means Special Forces generals are almost never going to command the main effort on the battlefield. They will either go to the conventional side of the fence or they will stay put and run the schoolhouse.

The Special Forces commander at Ft. Bragg, the one in charge of all Special Forces throughout the Army, does not go to war. Even though he may have been very successful as a captain, major, lieutenant colonel, and colonel, per the Nunn-Cohen agreement, he stays where he can train and develop more Special Forces.

Instead of continuing to command Special Forces in the field like an Eisenhower or a Bradley, the Special Force generals at Ft. Bragg are tasked to continue producing Special Forces captains, majors, lieutenant colonels, and colonels for all of the Special Forces Groups. That means that those forces that deploy to combat and conduct unconventional warfare will always stay at a tactical level because the command is not

This photograph shows an SF NCO (in black baseball cap) using an interpreter with ID card around his neck to teach the indig platoon leader the basics of maneuvering a platoon. Notice the stone wall in the background. I once told a village elder that the stonework in his village was beautiful, thinking my neighbors back home would love to have such stonework. He replied, "Yes, we are very poor and cannot afford cement."

Top: Here an SF trooper teaches the basics of "fire and maneuver." The gravel upon which they lie was not put there as a parking lot; it is simply what much of what Afghanistan looks like up close. *Above:* Just outside the gates at one of our A-Camps, these Afghan Guards learned how to attack and defend. Within three weeks, these men were recruited, trained, and organized, and began running combat patrols against the terrorists in their valley. One dozen Americans and about 400 indigenous troopers can clean out a valley if given the green light.

at the general officer rank. The law practically negates any unconventional capability at the strategic level.

These scenarios that we've talked about — Lware, Asabadad and many, many more not mentioned — are *tactical* successes, illustrating the power of unconventional warfare and what the "road not taken" could be on the strategic level — i.e., a *national* level.

But most in the special operations community are not Special Forces, and therefore they are not *unconventional warfare—*focused. Most in this community have a focus on conventional counterterrorist actions or unilateral actions. All are patriots and warriors but few of them are Special Forces soldiers with decades of unconventional warfare experience behind them, and so they don't naturally get it. They don't see how this patient, local approach can pay off the same way a quick, violent combat strike does, but with permanent, nation-changing results. This fact becomes pertinent when those same generals become the commanding generals of our combat operations in a place like Afghanistan, or become key leaders in Washington. The best answer is to work *by, with and through* the indigenous population for permanent change at a strategic level: to train the locals to take care of their problems themselves, to give them the tools for lasting change and lasting security. Unfortunately, that often is not how conventional military leaders think.

I liken this to an American football team playing soccer. America clearly has great *American* football players. We have leagues of great blockers and tacklers. We can pass and catch better than anyone. The enemy, however, is playing soccer (another kind of football). Soccer has no need for blocking and tackling and quarterbacks, yet these are the tactics our top leaders know. We can try to muscle our way through that game, but when we give up and go home, the game of soccer goes on unchanged.

When we leave Afghanistan, the conventional guys will have blown up their targets, but we unconventional guys would have learned to play soccer and would have worked by, with and through, and thus we would leave behind a population who knew how to fight on their own. That's how to deny the Taliban unfettered freedom to operate in Afghanistan long after we're gone. *By, with and through.*

When I presented the Afghan National Guard concept to the commanding general of Combined Forces Command in Afghanistan, I was trying to take UW from the tactical to the strategic level.

The ultimate answer we got was no. Good idea, but we can't afford the $5 a day to pay those soldiers.

The pay for an Afghan National Army (ANA) soldier was much less than five U.S. dollars a day, and the higher headquarters did not want to upset the apple cart. So for now, the main effort in this war on terrorism was going to continue to be the U.S. Army's unilateral operations.

OK. Back to the drawing boards.

My mission and the mission of my task force was pretty simple — to transform Afghanistan from being a safe haven for Al-Qaeda to at least being a neutral nation in the fight against terror, which was the same objective as the other Special Operations task forces, made up of Rangers and SEALs and their supporting helicopters from the 160th Special Operations Aviation Regiment.

But there was a major conceptual difference in our methods. One method was to fight this enemy *by, with and through* the indigenous population. The other method was to kill or capture the enemy in general, and Osama bin Laden and any other of his major lieutenants we could get our hands on.

Of course one of the things that every Westerner in Afghanistan was asking about concerned the whereabouts of Osama Bin Laden. From a tactical and operational level, his whereabouts, I would argue, were not the first priority. We were pretty certain bin Laden was in West Waziristan—the area I talked about on the Pakistan-Afghan border — but Waziristan was more of a tribal area than a national area. The people in those areas consider themselves their own little nations, and therefore they had no particular allegiances to any governments, including Afghanistan or Pakistan. Bin Laden was more of a folk hero. He had been neutralized as a field commander; he was not in operational control of his force and he hadn't been for years.

When I was in command in Afghanistan, I often thought that we may never know what happened to him or we may find him tomorrow. Either way, bin Laden has been largely only a symbolic leader for several years. I thought that at the end of the day, we may simply realize that he died at the bottom of some cave like a snake, never to be heard from again. As it turned out, of course, our great SEALs tracked him down in Pakistan and finished that chapter of the war with cold steel. What a great day for America, symbolic or not, when bin Laden went to meet his maker!

Yet, as we made our rounds and talked to the leaders about the situations in their villages and about the situation with Al-Qaeda and what we can do to motivate their citizens to fight against terrorists, we asked people we were visiting, "Where is bin Laden? What do you think he and his lieutenants are doing?" At about the same time, the U.S. government increased the bounty on bin Laden from $25 million to $50 million. Now that's a *bounty*, meaning dead or alive, and in America, if you had a $50 million bounty on *your* head you'd better hide very carefully because that will buy you a lot of enemies.

If I were to tell an American he or she might get $50 million, he or she would start thinking about houses, cars, vacations, toys, things we could do with $50 million. U.S. $50 million is a foreign currency and, in fact, the *idea* of currency to these Afghans is relatively foreign.

I'll never forget, as we were describing this to one of the Afghan leaders, the one question he had. *How many goats can you buy for $50 million?* Our immediate answer was *virtually every goat between here and the Mediterranean.* Afghans simply look for money to be translated into basics: Food, water, shelter. *How can $50 million increase my survivability?* In this rugged country with unforgiving terrain and weather, we would probably get more help by simply offering 200 goats. The Afghans' motivation isn't the $50 million, but surviving.

Conventional military operators and thinkers may believe that all guerrilla forces are comprised of fighters that simply need to be out-fought. This is not the case in Afghanistan.

Early in my Special Forces training, I was exposed to Mao Tse-tung's 1937 book *On Guerrilla Warfare*, which he wrote as a manual to help the Chinese fight against the Japanese, using guerrilla tactics that he had learned and successfully practiced for over a decade. What I took from that book is that an insurgency actually has three levels of insurgents: the guerrillas, the auxiliaries, and the underground members. Each has different roles, capabilities, and motivations. But each also has its own limitations, weaknesses, and vulnerabilities.

The guerrilla is the armed fighter. He carries the weapons, lives in the field, and conducts operations full time. He is the one we most clearly identify as "the enemy." Depending on what phase of the insurgency the Taliban was in, it was possible that as few as 10 percent of the Taliban could be called active "guerrillas." Within the guerrilla ranks, some were hardened Taliban fighters who needed to be killed and others were simply unemployed peasants with few real options in life.

The second level, the auxiliary, provides support and guidance to the guerrilla fighters. An auxiliary member may pick up a weapon and fight, but he usually feeds the guerrillas, helps arm them, and provides strategic level guidance. Guerrilla leaders are the ones to set up specific ambushes or raids, but the auxiliary leaders are the ones to tell them where to focus their efforts, e.g., in a specific region or province or perhaps for a specific period of time.

Finally, the underground member is the least involved member of the insurgency. He provides the raw materials such as money, food, or information. Farmers may give (voluntarily or not) a portion of their food crops to the auxiliary for distribution to the guerrillas during campaigning. Underground members are, at a minimum, looking the other way when guerrillas prepare for their operations and move through their areas. On the other hand, they may actively seek out and pass along valuable information about anti-insurgency operations such as my operations or the NATO operations.

With this understanding, the challenge is to identify, by region or by individual, who and where the various members of the insurgency are. We knew that in some regions of the country we'd get shot at as we patrolled through a valley: those were clearly guerrilla-held regions.

In other neighborhoods we'd only get rocks thrown at us if we were not ignored completely. Were those neighborhoods highly populated by auxiliary or underground members?

Insurgencies don't issue ID cards. There are no rosters of members—no annual subscriptions drives or anything of the sort—so we really needed to be able to gauge the popular feelings of an area and of the individuals.

We began to produce a GAU (Guerrillas, Auxiliary, Underground) Template. This was a map that we'd color-code by regions to indicate

I saw a few Afghan girls below the age of about 6 or 8. Older girls are all sequestered in their family compound for the duration of their lives, unless supervised by a family member while going to the market. Oddly enough, the young girls I saw were often dressed in pretty and colorful outfits.

guerrillas, underground, and/or auxiliary members. Then, based on the motivation and capabilities of the insurgents, we would target that region with an appropriate weapon system, be it kinetic or non-kinetic.

In a guerrilla region, we may need to use force as the predominant weapon of choice — with Afghan combat forces leading the way, of course.

In an auxiliary-heavy community, we may need some form of civil affairs activity, like schools or health clinics to get the population to our side.

One of our most worthwhile and successful means of bringing the fence-sitters to the side of democracy and away from the Taliban was by setting up medical clinics and addressing some of the physical needs of the local population. At almost every A-camp, the SF medic would set up a formal clinic or hold "sick call hours" for locals to come with their ailments. These medics saw everything from colds to childbirths to gunshot wounds to car wreck victims to sick donkeys. Whenever possible, we'd hire (and pay) local doctors or nurses to work at these clinics as well (*by, with and through* is always good). In most parts of Afghanistan, the local health care was so atrocious that an aspirin would take most Afghan families 500 years forward in medical technology.

At one clinic, we performed some impressive surgery. We were in the Konar district with the 19th Special Forces Group operating a clinic in a mud hut. The medic was a National Guardsman and a high school science teacher in his civilian profession. He had taken a one-year leave of absence from teaching when he was deployed to Afghanistan. I know he had some stories to tell his students when he got home after a year. Some high school in Utah is lucky to have that science teacher.

One morning, a father brought his five-or six-year-old daughter into the clinic. She was missing her left thumb and index finger. Only minutes before, her hand had been caught between two cars as they crashed into each other, leaving her with two traumatically amputated appendages. After hours of surgery in a mud hut on the edge of our A-camp, this wonderful SF medic, with the assistance of one of his teammates, was able to reattach the index finger. The thumb was crushed beyond use, so he attached the finger to the muscles and tendons originally belonging to the thumb so that the child would be able to grasp things with the dexterity associated with a thumb.

This story highlights several points: first, Special Forces medics are highly trained and capable of performing advanced medical procedures in environments that would astonish most doctors. Second, the fact that a father brought his daughter to see us indicates that our troops had earned their trust. Little known to most Americans back home, not only were we outsiders in Afghanistan, but we were often derisively called "rich Russians"—not a good thing.

In order to unite the locals against the American soldiers, the Taliban claimed that we were just like the Russians. Americans have helicopters like the Russians, armored vehicles like the Russians, we look like the Russians. We just have more money than the Russians. Perhaps the only thing that unites all Afghans is their hatred for the Russians. But this man with his daughter in his arms can now say that these Americans are not like the Russians.

This concept, repeated one valley at a time, one patient at a time, is the way to win over the locals. There is no blitzkrieg with this kind of war. Patience and persistence are the answer.

Remember, in all areas of this unconventional approach to warfare, the key is to get the indigenous to do the heavy lifting. One of the advantages of working with Afghani forces is that they know, or can figure out faster than we can, who is an active guerrilla and who may be sitting on the fence as a passive member of the auxiliary. They can identify the motivation of each and thus appropriately target that motivation. The targeting may be with old-fashioned fire and steel, or with a more indirect mix of information, diplomacy, and economic power.

This type of analysis, of course, is very complex and time-consuming. GAU templates can change weekly. This effort takes the entire foreign military forces to focus on not only fighting the active insurgent (guerrilla), but on fighting the reasons for the insurgency as well.

If done well and across the country, this way of unconventional thinking can separate the guerrilla from the people. That separation must be physical as well as fiscal, social and philosophical. If the guerrilla is out in the cold (literally and theoretically), he will eventually die on the vine. That is an unconventional approach to this war, and the road to success in this war. As I said, we don't want to kill all of the fish, we just want to change the temperature of the water and make it inhospitable for the terrorists.

30

Bases, Good Order
and Discipline

I really had a mini-city in my headquarters (HQ). Almost a society. It was not a homogenous group; it included lawyers and finance and bookkeepers and counselors, and soldiers and surgeons and chefs and cooks, all buying supplies from the locals. We got most of our food from big refrigerated units shipped out of Europe, but we got some off the local economy. So we had veterinarians who would inspect any food that we bought from locals to make sure it wasn't contaminated or infected with gangrene. Our vets also would go out with the SF A-teams and do a medical clinic for goats and camels and horses. You heal a warlord's child and he likes you; you strengthen his herd of goats and he LOVES you.

There are certain scheduled flights for logistics of all kinds. About twice a day there's a mail bird coming in from Europe. The mail would go to an Army post office at Bagram. The Army is the executive agent for military mail. That means that even in a "joint" environment like the JTF, the Army runs the post offices. One of my good friends from my time at the Marine Corps University at Quantico once said that they spell "joint" (as in interservice) A-R-M-Y.

Every two days there's a food bird coming in from Europe. We also had what we called a ring flight that the JTF would run with conventional helicopters that would run all the camps once a week.

So if you were at A-camp Blessing — maybe every two weeks because it was a small camp with a difficult LZ — every other Thursday you got the helicopter. Camp Blessing was named for 75th Ranger Regiment Sergeant Blessing, who was killed not far from there.

167

What you see is based on where you sit. This U.S. Army helicopter crewman's helmet reflects the wild mountain ranges of the Hindu Kush.

That's when you got your mail; that's when you got your chow resupply, unless it was an emergency; that's when everything came. So if you needed something, you'd get it on the next ring flight in two weeks.

Unless it was an emergency, in which case we'd obviously adjust and make a special trip. But Afghanistan is so big from top to bottom, that's a five-or six-hour trip in a helicopter. Typically a ring flight would consist of a couple of Chinooks and a couple of Apache gunships.

The JTF air and logistical planners would mix up the route and timing a little bit so that the bad guys wouldn't realize, "Hey, they're going to be here at 10:00 tomorrow morning like they are every Thursday." And we'd tell people that their next ring "Thursday" flight is actually going to be Wednesday night. You've got to alter your routine because the bad guys have time to wait and identify patterns.

Never assume unsophisticated or illiterate equates to stupid. The enemy would think nothing of having a little kid sit there and every time that helicopter comes, to write down the time.

An old Afghan once said to me, "Americans have all the watches, but we have all the time." And they do have all the time. We're thinking, "What can I do in six months?" and they're thinking, "What will happen in 50 years?"

As a Special Forces commander, I had very few discipline problems, because again, everybody busted his tail to get into the Regiment. When I was a battalion commander at Ft. Carson, we all lived on "Colonels Row." The other commanders and I all had our individual Regimental crests on the door to show what unit we had. I kept my battalion crest and it is on my barn door right now.

At Carson, after work I'd come home and meet my conventional battalion commander neighbors over the fence with a beer and we'd talk about what we did that day. I had an infantry battalion commander and an engineer battalion commander that I was buddies with. They lived right next to me. Awesome guys, great families, wives and kids. Folks wonder what makes soldiers different. Walk down a street like that on any Army fort and you'd get a good idea.

One of the things I learned from these guys was that Wednesday night was UCMJ night, Uniform Code of Military Justice. That was when they, as the commander, would oversee court for anybody that's in their battalion and therefore subject to UCMJ. They did that every Wednesday night. Every Wednesday night they had five or six young troopers who were in some sort of trouble — late for formation, got drunk, told a sergeant to take a hike. The vast majority of the infractions were fairly minor, of course, but five or six came up each week.

In my two years of battalion command I had only two. Two UCMJ events in two years. Now "minor" is a relative term. If you don't show up for work, it's a criminal offense in the Army. If you don't show up for work as a civilian, you get fired. If you don't show up to work in the Army, you go to jail. As a civilian if you tell your boss to take a hike, you get fired. In the Army if you tell your boss to take a hike, you go to jail. It's just different.

So my conventional commander counterparts would hold court every Wednesday night. They would have five or six legal issues a week.

In two years of battalion command, I had only two cases of discipline problems. Special Forces Soldiers simply don't have many problems.

The bad news is when they did have a problem, it was typically not an "I overslept for formation" kind of problem.

I had one of my support company soldiers (not an SF trooper, but a mechanic in my SF battalion), come to me and say, "Hey, sir, I'd like for you to sign my leave for three weeks." The rule is: any leave request longer than two weeks, the colonel had to sign it. Two weeks or less the company commander could sign it. Two weeks or more, I signed it. "Okay, what are you doing for three weeks?" "Well sir, I've got to go to jail." I said, "What?!" He said, "Yes sir, I got arrested six months ago for public intoxication and I've got a three-week jail term. So I've got to go to jail." So I gave him a three-week vacation and he went to jail.

I did have one SF Soldier who was arrested and charged for raping his wife. I adjudicated it as the law requires and gave him the option to receive the most significant punishment I was authorized to dispense, or if he wanted to plead innocent, to accept trial by court-martial. So he elected to go to a court-martial. In the end, he was not found guilty, predominantly because of the lack of evidence. "He said, she said." And who knows? Like the rest of this society, you are innocent until proven guilty in our country.

When I was in Afghanistan I think I had about three discipline problems. So again, 4,000 people, deployed in a high stress area for a year and only three problems—that is pretty good. The general order number one in Afghanistan is: no drinking, no sex and no souvenirs. And of course those are the three things every soldier wants to do. The only vice I could enjoy in Afghanistan was smoking some good Cuban cigars.

One Soldier did get in trouble for drinking. We got a call one morning from the MP's at Bagram saying they had arrested one of my national guard support Soldiers for, of all things, DUI! He'd taken one of our military vehicles to the tent of a friend in another unit and gotten drunk, slept the rest of the night, and then driven back to my HQ in the morning. An MP at the security gate saw him swerve this HMMV and pulled him over. Of all the things I expected to see in combat, that was not one of them. I busted that sergeant down one strip and sent him home with a letter of reprimand.

Another soldier, a company commander from the Army Reserve, got in trouble for drinking and sex. I relieved that officer of command and sent her home in disgrace. Apparently, a couple of nights before I took the colors (a couple of nights before I took command), one of my coalition forces from Europe teamed up with one of the companies from the Army Reserve to have a big party. Who knows where they got so much booze, but they got it.

After I took command and heard about the party and the accompanying shenanigans, I conducted an investigation. We found cases and cases of booze hidden behind a false wall in the company headquarters. The commander, whom I soon relieved, clamed ignorance of the whole thing. I'm not sure if she was ignorant or complacent, but she was certainly unsuited to command a company in combat. So she went home with a letter of reprimand.

One officer, a National Guardsman, later got in trouble for trying to smuggle some captured enemy weapons home at the end of the deployment, in a storage container with the other unit gear. I didn't hear about that until we had all been home for several months. I knew he was a gun collector and thus was highly covetous of the many captured weapons we had around our headquarters. When his unit was packing their gear to come home, I reminded him that he and his guys had done a good job and for him to be careful and watch out for any stupid attempts to bring home weapons. Guess he did not listen. Only one of these three was a Special Forces soldier, but like I said, they don't get in trouble much, but when they do it is not for sleeping in and missing any early morning formation.

The final aspect of discipline in the military is sexual activity. I use the word discipline on purpose because this is not a moral issue or a lifestyle critique but an issue of military discipline. Let me explain.

What is the mission of the world's most powerful military? In short, we exist to fight and win America's wars. Any change in military policies should only be enacted if that change helps the military better execute its mission: winning America's wars. Liberal politicians, academics and many thoughtful people will tell you that good leadership can overcome any challenges, including this one. As an Army colonel with 24 years experience in leading our soldiers in almost every possible situation, I will argue ... they are right. Good leadership can overcome almost any challenge.

With good leadership, starving men low on ammunition still fought at Valley Forge and later won our independence. With good leadership the 101st Airborne Division fought their way out of Bastogne during the Battle of the Bulge, even though they were outnumbered, outgunned, and outsupplied. I'm continually amazed at what challenges good soldiers and good leaders can overcome. Our history books are full of examples of leaders overcoming challenges.

For my last combat tour I commanded 4,000 men and women of the Combined Joint Special Operations Task Force all over Afghanistan for a year. I used every leadership tool in my tool bag: mental, physical, emotional, and spiritual. By using these skills and by the grace of God I was able to bring most—most—of the Americans home in one piece. But I can assure you that I did not need any additional challenges that had to be overcome by good leadership. The Taliban and Al-Qaeda provided me plenty of challenges. I needed my president and his policies to reduce those challenges, not add to them.

I expect that I am one of the very few American commanders who has actually commanded openly gay soldiers in combat before the policy change—not American soldiers, but Afghans. For some reason in the Afghan culture, women are seen as so unclean and untouchable that men often turn a blind eye to homosexual activity and see it as a better option than shaming a family by being with a woman.

I remember one Thursday night, the night before the Islamic holy day, while at one of the Special Forces A-Camps along the border. Several of the SF NCOs jokingly called it "Man-Love Thursday." After dinner, as the sun began to set, I watched Afghan soldiers change out their guards on the perimeter of our little A-Camp. I saw two Afghan soldiers walk out to their LP/OP holding hands. Now I know that Americans have a different view of men holding hands than other cultures do. I also know what two young lovers look like. I looked at the SF captain I was standing with. He read my mind. "Man-Love Thursday, sir. We find them out there every week doing ... well you can imagine." As far as I know, we never got attacked when two lovers were stationed at the same spot in the perimeter but it is one additional challenge I'd prefer our leaders not be saddled with.

31

Holiday Festivities

Each of us has special holiday memories. In my family, holidays seem to be right out of a Norman Rockwell painting. From my earliest memories Thanksgiving, Christmas, Easter — all of them bring back good recollections.

I spent several holidays overseas. Each of them brings back a special memory. I spent one Thanksgiving in Bosnia. As a young major I was in the CJSOTF located in an old hotel on the outskirts of Sarajevo. The mess hall for the small CJSOTF staff was the bar in the old Herzegovina Hotel. In the semi-ruined hotel compound, with the cold wet Balkan winter in its early stages, the multi-nation staff gathered around for hot turkey, dressing and all the fixings. We had Americans, Brits, Canadians, all the members of the coalition staff.

While in Afghanistan, I spent Thanksgiving at one of the A-camps. As the commander, I had my logistics officer brief me every day for a week prior to each holiday on the status of getting hot turkey to the out-stations. So I had Thanksgiving dinner in the most remote of American outstations, an A-camp deep in the Hindu Kush. It amazes me to this day that our nation has the wherewithal and the passion to deliver such wonderful meals to such forsaken locations. We do this because the focus for our Army has always been the soldier — not the gear, not the logistics, but the soldier.

For Christmas season in Afghanistan, my staff decorated the mess hall with a plastic Christmas tree and as many holiday decorations as we could make or get mailed to us. They collected CDs with Christmas music. Our chaplain put together a couple of chorus presentations of popular Christmas carols. The night of our CJSOTF holiday party our cooks prepared a feast fit for kings. They had all of our favorite dishes ready to go and presented with such flair that the finest restaurants in New York could have learned something.

By chance, one of the officers assigned to our HQ had an excellent voice. She sang a couple of faith-based Christmas songs for us that, I am sure, touched the soul of everyone there. We listened to her golden voice and ate our magnificent dinner around the Christmas tree. Somehow, most of us managed to find red Santa hats. While certainly not in accordance with military uniform regulations, I too sported my own Santa hat, with airborne wings on the front — Airborne!

Each of us missed our family back home, yet I think each of us also realized we were blessed on this Christmas day to be in the company of heroes. Even more blessed to be invested in something important, fighting for freedom and liberating the oppressed. Good Christmas gifts.

On Easter of that year, we had a sunrise service. Of note is that we had the service on the roof of our motor pool building. That building had the largest, flattest and most stable roof in our CJSOTF compound. Interestingly, that building was originally built by the Soviets when they occupied that part of Afghanistan. The Soviets, of course, with their communist form of government, believed that religion is the opium of the masses. As Karl Marx originally said, "Die Religion ... ist das Opium des Volkes," indicating that religion and the freedom to practice it is an addictive lifestyle that should be avoided. Therefore, we worshiped our Lord as he brought the sun onto the horizon that Easter morning, and we sang with particular gusto from the roof of the old Soviet building. I am sure the Russian construction workers never envisioned such an event when they built it years ago.

Later that year, on Memorial Day weekend, we lost four great Americans to a command-detonated explosive device. It was 29 May 2004. Every Memorial Day I recall, with special understanding, the cost of our freedom.

Memorial Day, the last Monday in May, was originally called "Decoration Day." On that day, Southern ladies and Southern school children would decorate the graves of the Confederate dead. In more modern history, the custom grew to honor all the soldiers our nation has lost over the past 235 or so years.

When I was young, I realized that the soldiers who died while gaining and then defending our freedom had paid the ultimate price. Like many Americans I believed that those fallen warriors of the past wars bought the freedom that the rest of us enjoy.

I realized, after seeing several great Americans pay that price, that we can never really *buy* freedom. No matter how much we pay, no matter how many soldiers ultimately die while defending our Constitution, we will never fully *own* these freedoms. You see, when you own something, it is yours forever. When you own a house or any property, you can pass it along to future generations. It is yours and theirs to use forever. No more payments are required.

But with freedom, future payments will always be required. Soon after we are no longer willing to pay for our freedom, we will lose it. General Eisenhower said, "History does not long entrust the care of freedom to the weak or the timid." Thus, our great patriots who died for our freedom did not buy it for the future generations. They only *rented* our freedom. We are free to enjoy that freedom as long as we pay the rent. Like renting a house or a car, we can consider it our own only as long as we make the payments. The true owner of the house or car can and will repossess it as soon as we miss mailing the check. Similarly, others will take possession of our freedom the day we show the world we are no longer willing to pay for it with the efforts of our best.

Those are the recollections of this veteran each Memorial Day.

32

Political Correctness

Warfare is ultimately a string of decisions at the tactical, operational, and strategic levels, decisions about what to do and when to do it. Some decisions are made from the military perspective. Some decisions are made out of political necessity. When those two perspectives conflict, the political perspective always wins, and that's the way it should be. As Prussian military philosopher Carl von Clausewitz taught in the early 1800s, war is simply a continuation of politics by other means. However, some decisions are made not out of political necessity, but political correctness. And that causes great concern.

A case in point. When President Barack Obama gave his presentation on the Afghan strategy at the U.S. Military Academy in the fall of 2009, he failed to use a couple of words that are very important terms in the realm of military strategy. He never used the words *victory* or *win*. He simply used the phrase *ending the war on a positive note*. Years later, we are seeing the culmination of that strategy with no actual victory at hand.

When you talk about war, diplomacy has broken down and the arguments of two nations are now being decided with guns and bullets. In war, victory is the objective.

Second, he never properly identified the enemy: *Muslim extremists*. We're fighting Muslim extremists. We're not fighting Baptist extremists. We're not fighting radical Presbyterians. We're not fighting eco-terrorists. We're fighting Muslim extremists.

I believe the reason he used the term "violent extremists" as opposed to Muslim extremists is because he didn't want to offend Muslims. Yet step one in identifying a solution is always defining and understanding the problem. Remember my "leadership-comes-down-to-golf" theory? Defining the situation correctly is key.

Soon after 9/11, President Bush identified this war as the *Global War on Terror*. There are a couple of key words there. A *global* war implies that we will search down the enemy anywhere, anytime, anyplace. And it's a global *war*, not a global police activity.

Soon after President Obama's election, however, he changed that phrase so that when soldiers are deployed to war their orders no longer read *in support of a global war on terror*, as my orders read when I went to Afghanistan. Instead, soldiers' orders now read *in support of global contingency operations*. While these are simple words, the difference in a military order has a huge impact. We're telling our soldiers they're no longer fighting a global war against terror. Now it's simply "contingency operations," whether it's Afghanistan or Iraq or Haiti or tsunami support in the Pacific.

When we fight a global *war* on terror, terrorists are treated as prisoners of war and not criminals. What's the difference, you ask? The difference is that in war, the objective of taking prisoners is not justice. The objective is to gather operational intelligence, to keep the enemy off the battlefield, and to ultimately use them to win the war.

In peacetime crime-fighting, the objective is simply justice. In my command, we didn't even use the term POW, prisoner of war. The POWs we captured in Afghanistan were called PUCs: persons under control. To have a POW, one had to have a "war." POWs have certain rights that we did not want to offer to these terrorist enemies.

Perhaps one of the most challenging things for Westerners when we work with Muslims is the concept of *Inshallah*. The phrase *Inshallah* is Arabic for *if Allah wills it.* Many of the Muslim officers I've worked with use that phrase almost as a punctuation mark, like a period or comma. *Yes, we will be there, Inshallah. We will practice and improve our marksmanship, Inshallah. We will find all of the Al-Qaeda this month, Inshallah.* It is a fatalistic philosophy.

One time, when I was getting a briefing from one of the many non–American components within the CJSOTF, specifically one of our Arab allies, the Inshallah mindset almost put me over the edge. Even the most flexible and culturally sensitive SF officers are often tempted to give in to our Type-A personalities.

It became clear to me during this briefing that the key phase of the operation was a linkup between one of the Special Forces A-teams and the company from the one of the three Arab or Central Asian contingencies. Any professional soldier knows that the most dangerous phase of many combat operations is linkup, because if either of the two forces gets confused or lost and begins shooting, fratricide will most certainly be the outcome.

On this particular operation, we needed the American SF team and the Arab infantry company to link up at a precise time and precise location. They could not be ten minutes late or early, nor could they be 500 meters off. Right place and right time. Period. As I listened to the plan I began to drill down to the details.

"Are you sure you can get right there," I asked Captain Mohamed as I pointed to a village on the map, "at exactly the right time?"

"Yes, yes, Inshallah, we will be there," he insisted. I said to him, "No *Inshallah*, captain. You must ensure you *are* there. No matter what. You must be exactly there and on time so that no one gets hurt."

He eventually agreed to be there, no matter what. I suspected that his concession was more to get me off his back than his actual guarantee to be there on time. With that understanding, I spoke to the American SF captain who was to make the discussed linkup. We agreed that he and his team would begin to monitor the location and direction of their linkup partners well prior to the actual linkup time.

"Just be ready to meet them in the general area and *about* the time we agreed to. Be flexible and stay in contact."

We agreed. The two teams from different worlds actually linked up more or less where and when we'd planned. Inshallah.

One of the words I learned not to use in planning was "hope." Any time a young officer briefed his plan to me with something like, "Sir, we hope to attack the enemy along this route," or "We hope to be at the rally point by 2400 hours tomorrow," my reaction was always, "Well, I *hope* I win the lottery, but if I don't then how will I *ensure* I make the financial objective?" Or sometimes, depending on the situation, I'd say, "What resources or guidance do you need from me to ensure your hope turns into reality?" "Hope" is not a course of action; it's just something to dream about. Ironically, "hope" was one of the key terms in a recent presidential race.

33

Afghan and
Pakistan Meetings

It is too easy for Westerners to think that all Muslims are alike, and vice versa. It is a natural human tendency to stereotype groups. Like any group of people, Muslims have several sub-groups, with different opinions, cultures and goals. Just like Christians, Jews or Hindus, some Muslims get along with each other, and some do not.

Nowhere was this more evident to me than in one of my monthly meetings along the Afghan-Pakistan border. Every month or so, I'd go with the local Afghan commander and his American Special Forces counterpart to a meeting with their counterpart from the Pakistan border guards. Our goal was to facilitate the Afghans and Pakistanis working together to control the joint border area.

The first Afghan commander I accompanied was from near one of our camps along the border. He was simply called "the Colonel." The Colonel took with him what he called "one company" of his soldiers. "Company" indicates specific organization and strength; I'd simply say "several" of his soldiers. He had fought against the Soviets and was a truly hardened combat veteran. I expect his hands and feet have been callused since early childhood. I never saw in him any sign of weakness.

One cold winter day, I asked how his soldiers were doing. We Americans had on our polypropylene long underwear, our Gortex outer wear, our nice warm boots and plenty of warm coffee. His men shared an old blanket between two men, both wearing cotton pants and a shirt. At about 10,000 feet in the mountains, we had a piercing cold wind. Weren't his men cold?

Top: COL Herd meets with local Afghan commanders from one of the indigenous and friendly forces (not of the Afghan National Army) prior to a meeting with the Pakistani military along the border. *Above:* We knew this man as Colonel "Gafar"; we did not know his real name. He was one of the most seasoned combat commanders I have ever met. He worked with our SF teams along the border and had probably been fighting UW in Afghanistan since he was a teenager.

The Colonel looked at me in wonderment and said, "Of course they are cold; it is winter. We'll warm up in the spring."

About 300 meters before we got to this border crossing point, we came across a company of Pakistani soldiers, but they were on the Afghan side of the border. One thing of particular personal concern was that all of their weapons were aimed at us. They had in effect moved a company-sized invasion force inside the borders of Afghanistan. I stood in the middle of the road telling the Pakistani commander, Colonel Saddam (no relation to the Iraqi dictator, he assured me), that he had to get his soldiers onto his side of the border.

Meanwhile, the Afghan Colonel was about to deploy his Afghan soldiers into a more aggressive formation.

This was high-stakes diplomacy. I got a very clear, and longer than I enjoyed, view of the business end of several RKGs and old soviet PKM machine guns. The PKM is a 7.62mm weapon produced in the 1960s and in use all over the world with a maximum effective range of about 1500

This Pakistani colonel commanded a brigade of the frontier guards. Note his recently trimmed hair and mustache. The uniform and insignia are distinctly British. He even carried a "swagger stick." In contrast, behind him is one of the officers of the Afghan forces we worked with. He had on his only clean uniform and wore no insignia.

meters. I was looking down their barrels from about 30 meters. I was the "duck" in the sitting duck scenario.

Sadam assured me that he was here to provide my team and me with protection.

"Then why are your weapons all pointing at me and my team?" I asked.

After much discussion, we were able to agree to move another 300 meters east, to the actual border (where Sadam already had a tent and meeting place set up). Both companies of soldiers, Afghan and Pakistani, set up a perimeter around our meeting place.

The Afghan and Pakistani commanders, the Special Forces company commander, and I sat down at the table to discuss the one real issue of the day: how can we work together to stop Al-

Only moments after this photograph, I was informed that "not one Al-Qaeda came from Pakistan, they all came from Afghanistan!" A couple of months later, after several attempts by Al-Qaeda to kill his nation's president, he admitted "perhaps a few" are in Pakistan.

Qaeda from crossing back and forth across the border?

The two commanders were as different as night and day. The Afghan was darkly tanned with a relatively long black beard. While he looked clean, I doubt he'd had an actual shower in a long time. He had a scar across his left cheek. His hands, and I expect his whole body, were tough like leather. His uniform was a new set of camouflaged fatigues with an insignia that resembled the old Soviet insignia. I'd never seen him wear another uniform. He was a fighter who was an expert in fighting, using multiple kinds of weapons, killing and leading men.

The Pakistani looked like a caricature of an officer from the old British Empire, except with darker skin. He had a beautifully trimmed handlebar mustache. His uniform was recently pressed, with several rows of ribbons on his chest. He wore fatigue pants and boots, yet his uniform blouse was a long flowing Tumbaan that my guys called a "man dress." It resembles a man's dress shirt that comes to the knees and is not tucked in.

He carried a wooden riding crop or "swagger stick" with silver tips on both ends. I could smell the faint odor of his cologne and would bet he had just recently finished a nicely cooked breakfast. He had at least a squad of men dedicated to serving tea and cookies to our little party in the tent in the Hindu Kush Mountains along the frontier border.

After tea and mutual compliments, we got down to the actual business of the day: how can we (Afghanistan, Pakistan and U.S.) close the border to Al-Qaeda and the Taliban? For the past two years Al-Qaeda and the Taliban had been using Pakistan as a safe haven where they would rest and train and from which they could attack the Afghan and coalition forces.

The Afghan commander described several encounters when he and his soldiers had been attacked, only to have their attackers quickly flee back across the border into Pakistan. Frequently, the Pakistani border guards would even watch as the fighters crossed back from west to east into Pakistan.

Colonel Sadam quickly and adamantly denied these accusations of allowing terrorists safe haven in Pakistan. "There is not one Al-Qaeda or Taliban terrorist in Pakistan!" he announced as he held his right index finger right in front of my face and then in the front of his Afghan counterpart's face. "Not even one!"

Belying this asserstion, over the next two months, Pakistani President (and retired General) Pervez Musharraf had two assassination attempts made upon his life by members of Al-Qaeda or Taliban terrorist organizations.

When we next met with Colonel Sadam a couple of months after our first meeting, he opened up the conversation with, "Perhaps there are a few terrorists inside of Pakistan." He sounded like a child who had just been caught with a hand in the cookie jar. "How can we work together to ensure our mutual peace?"

34

Prisoner Interrogation

I was in Afghanistan when the news broke about the Americans' handling of POWs at Abu Ghraib in Iraq.

The news and the political reaction it caused had huge repercussions among us warfighters. One immediate reaction came from the headquarters of the Combined Forces Command in Afghanistan with guidance to restrict our intelligence collection. Depending on the restrictions, a lack of timely and accurate intel would stop successful operations. At the very core of the *by, with and through* concept is gathering information through all types of locals.

Every professional soldier I know believes that torture is morally wrong and usually geo-politically foolish as well. Probably 80 percent to 90 percent of the POWs we captured would tell us everything they knew about ongoing operations as well as the structure and makeup of the insurgency without our having to apply significant stress. In most cases, all they really wanted was food, water and a warm blanket. Interestingly enough, most of the prisoners at the biggest POW holding cell in Afghanistan, at Bagram Airbase, gained about 15 pounds. All they did was eat, sleep and pray. So by providing basic creature comforts and some well-aimed questions, we were able to gain a great deal of actionable intelligence in a short time.

That is, in *most* cases. In some cases, the hardcore Muslim fanatic won't talk for food and water. So while torture itself is to be avoided, to clearly and publicly broadcast how we interrogate and at what point we will stop, is equally foolish.

If a prisoner who is already tired, scared and hungry does not know how far an interrogator will push, the fear of the unknown becomes a powerful motivator. However, if that same prisoner, well trained and hardcore, already knows exactly where we will stop an interrogation, then he has won the "I've got a secret" game.

One of my best interrogators was an Army National Guardsman specialist. By coincidence, she was also an attractive, young, athletic woman, perhaps 23 years old, about 5'8" with blonde hair and blue eyes.

I only describe this Soldier because in the gender- segregated Afghan society she used her gender to huge success in her interrogation work. Given their segregated background, in many cases the Taliban would be simply overcome and fall apart after being talked "to" by a woman. They reached "systems overload" on three accounts: one, they'd never seen an "uncovered" woman other than a family member; two, they had never seen a tall, blond, fit young American woman; and finally, they'd never had a woman in a position of authority over them. Add those three up and the walls just came tumbling down.

Some would say that to use cultural differences to create a stressful situation while interrogating prisoners is tantamount to "torture."

I say it is good interrogation.

35

Special Forces Soldiering

I liked two things most about the Army: the sense of camaraderie and the sense of purpose. I think most professionals are also motivated by the same two aspects of their profession. In the Army you are surrounded by people who have all passed the same tests, met the same standards and demands. In Special Forces it's a significant demand. You're on a team which others are trying to join, almost literally "dying to join." They have cleared almost insurmountable hurdles to be standing right there with you, and you cleared the same ones. From day one there's huge mutual respect and appreciation.

It's like the Olympic team. You've worked your whole life to be on that Olympic team.

In the career path of an Army officer you have a decision point at about three years after you've joined: either go SF or stay with your basic branch. Pretty cut-and-dried. Stay in the regular army or go to that window to make the leap. Obviously, the majority of professional soldiers choose to stay with their basic branch.

You also have a third choice: to get out.

That decision point comes at the end of your first tour, which for me came when I was deployed in the first Ranger Battalion on the Honduran-Nicaraguan border.

Little wonder that I missed the fact that my three-year window had arrived. I never thought about it. I just assumed I was in for life and it never crossed my mind that I had to re-up until I got back and I asked the 1st Sergeant where my paystub was. He said, "I don't know, sir. We didn't get one for you. Go down to the finance office and see where it is." So I went down to finance and said, "Hey, I am Lt. Herd. Where's my paystub?" And they went through the records and said, "Well, you got out of the Army a month ago." I said, "No, I didn't. I promise I was in Honduras a month ago and I'm still in the Army today." They said, "Okay, then there's a mistake."

So for a little while technically I was out of the Army, even though I didn't know it. It took about six months to get all the paperwork straightened out, and I eventually got the back pay as well. I had a little apartment that probably cost $500 a month. I was deployed so I didn't spend any money on groceries.

About six months after my return from the Honduras and Nicaraguan border (after I got back in the Army I never left), the decision point was at hand. I'd already done my basic branch tour and was "qualified" as an artilleryman. I'd been to the advanced course. The question was: Special Forces or not? I had a good enough record to make me believe I would be considered. I knew that I liked Special Operations. I loved the Rangers. I loved the people. I loved the culture.

Leaving the relative security of the conventional Army was a tough choice. I believe that you should push the envelope until you run out of space. And I kept pushing and kept finding space so it worked out well. There are certainly a lot of great things in the Army. I don't know that I would have been as happy had I stayed in the conventional Army for twenty years. I think I would have been successful, but I wouldn't have been as happy. It was me. And again, for me having grown up playing army, football, scouts and GI Joes and studying history, Special Forces was a perfect fit. There are so many common personality traits between the participants of those activities.

I said earlier two things kept me in the Army. One is the camaraderie and the second is the mission. You're doing something important. As I get older now and look around I realize that a lot of people spend their lives being successful at things that aren't inherently very important. And what a waste that would be to spend your life being successful at something that didn't matter. Soldiering matters and I believe I have somewhat of a talent for it. So that was a pleasure.

As I look at old soldiers through history, I feel the same camaraderie. If, through some magical time warp science-fiction thing, I were to travel backward in time, or if they were to go forward, I would click pretty well with most of the men in these old paintings, I believe, even though they may be from different cultures or maybe different points of view. But the personality traits, I think, are very similar.

I read a book years ago on Nathan Bedford Forrest, who made a comment that his headquarters were his time in the saddle. And that thinking really sank in with me because that means he didn't have a big field headquarters with flags and aides and staffs. Wherever he was at the gallop, that's where headquarters was. And that's something that I try to personify. Headquarters is not the building where the radio is, headquarters is my boots. Where my boots are, that's where headquarters is. That's aggressive, and that's the way I felt like I was meant to be.

I have an American flag on my front porch. It has lighting and never goes down. I think our country is a great country, predominantly because of individual courage over the last 235 or so years. Our country is not a strong country because of the strong central bureaucratic government, although at times that's worked. But if you look at the major milestones in our history — the colonization of the country, the westward movement — that's because individuals, really hard-working people, took it upon themselves and shouldered the risks and defied odds and came to this place called America at an extreme price. Individuals and families who put it on the line to reach their goals.

I think that trait of empowerment is what's made us great and I'm concerned because I fear that personality trait is waning and leaning toward a desire to have a big brother who will take care of you if you fall.

Don't get me wrong: I know we need a strong central government to marshal our forces as needed. One of the big differences between our military and most militaries of the world is a very clear subjugation of the military to civil authority. No one in our military is confused about the question of authority: ultimately it rests with our elected officials. We may or may not like a decision, and we may or may not like the politicians, and we make the same cynical comments about one thing or another that everybody else does. But at the end of the day, if the people speak and a commander-in-chief decides, it should happen. It will happen. And it will always happen.

And that's not the case, certainly, in third-world countries. And I think that is one of the reasons we're still a world power.

The oath I took all those years ago is still valid. I never disavowed that oath: *I will support and defend the Constitution of the United States against all enemies, foreign and domestic; that I will bear true faith and allegiance to the same; that I take this obligation freely, without any mental reservation or purpose of evasion; and that I will well and faithfully discharge the duties of the office on which I am about to enter. So help me God.*

There's a line in the middle of every decision in the military. On one side of that line is the time for discussion. On the other side of that line is the time for execution. Soldiers learn early on how to figure out which side of that line they're on.

We're all about discussion when you're on the appropriate side of that line. Counter to a lot of stereotypes, the military really brings in lots of discussion and ideas. And commanders take all that in. Good commanders listen to diverse opinions, not just everybody who thinks the same way. That's the real value in diversity. Not a skin color, gender, or social status factor, but a difference in thinking.

That's what makes organizations better. And then once the decision is made, the time for discussion is over. I have seen it in my military career, and I'm sure everybody has. Some people learn that point better than others. And it's frustrating when someone is still discussing the issue when you're already in the execution mode.

I've been on both ends of that. I've executed things that I didn't agree with but the rule is, as long as it's moral and legal, you do it. If it's immoral or illegal, then you stop.

Again, looking back across history, that was the central argument at Nuremburg. "I was just following orders" doesn't work. So the American military deliberately teaches leaders to "faithfully administer all legal orders given."

That's a discussion point — legal orders. I've told every subordinate I've ever had and every commander I've ever had has told me, if you come across a moral dilemma, you do the morally right thing.

If anybody says, I think we're in a moral dilemma and we can't go forward, that's when everybody takes a breath and reanalyzes and says,

"Okay, if this is really a moral problem then let's adjust." If you just don't get over or around the issue, then you just don't get it, or the order you are seeing is against the law. I've seen several folks who did not "get it." But I don't remember ever getting an order that was against a law.

This is not so much a moral dilemma, but I'll give you one example of a professional dilemma. In Afghanistan the JTF commander was re-missioning my headquarters from an unconventional headquarters to a regional command headquarters just like the infantry brigades.

While it was not immoral or illegal, the decision was extremely illogical and did not support victory, which I believe is a moral requirement. I pushed back really hard and ultimately wrote the letter to Ft. Bragg saying that this was in the process. Ft. Bragg called him and we had some serious general officer discussion going on.

So I kept the UW mission that my soldiers were uniquely qualified for, but I almost got relieved or fired from my command for going against my higher commander's intent. I felt extreme heat from my commander, who questioned my loyalty and my willingness to follow legal orders, right to my face. It was a bloody day but I felt it was so important that if one colonel has to fall on his sword, then so be it.

We got over it and ended on good terms. He's an outstanding commander and I think the world of him. And ultimately I was able to convince him that I was in fact loyal to the cause of freedom and the cause of victory and I was simply writing that letter to inform the SOCOM commander that his task of building and fielding UW forces like mine was being put at risk.

SOCOM is tasked to stand up unconventional forces and direct action forces. My force was created recruited, trained, organized and deployed to conduct unconventional warfare. That's my charter. That's what Congress mandated. That's what I do. If you re-task me to do something else, while it is legal, it is not in accordance with the intent and it will risk failure and I could not tolerate it.

When I was a child, the military in itself certainly wasn't pushed on me by my parents. But the sense of duty, honor and responsibility was. That initial sense of duty was magnified by my own experiences and study. I learned that God gave us gifts and we're expected to use them for the betterment of humanity, somehow. How you use that gift, or "talent" as the parable states, is irrelevant, as long as the talent is used, not wasted, and the glory is given to the Lord, not the holder of the talent.

I always thought Jesus' parable of the talents as told by Matthew was one of the most powerful in the Bible. In those days a talent was a monetary denomination, like a dollar or a French franc. I've heard its value is around 20 years' worth of day laborers' wages—significant! Yet even if we use the modern definition of talent, as a skill or special ability, the parable is still of great value. Perhaps it's even more relevant. God gave us talents, just as the master in the parable gave money to his servants. Both the master and the Lord expect something back from us.

The sooner we understand what our talents are and recognize our obligation to maximize them, the better. I feel that my talents involve leading people in complex and difficult tasks. In my case, the gift was being a soldier. I used that gift to be the best soldier I could be, and then tried to use that to lead honestly and in a purposeful fashion.

Now we all have to take stock and try to understand what our talents are, and how we can use them for a greater purpose. We're a constantly evolving species. We transition through stages in our lives. We must ask ourselves: are we making the best of the educational opportunities we have? Are we using our talents in the workplace? When you're on a business trip are you honest to your beliefs? Magnifying your talents to glorify God is the key no matter what walk of life you choose — in the Army or in civilian life.

36

Power in the
Modern Era

The four elements of power are: diplomatic, informational, military and economic. Every country has those four elements at some level or another and has had them since the beginning of the nation-state paradigm in modern history. Every conflict can ultimately be solved with application of one or a combination of those four elements.

World War II, for example, was primarily a military solution, yet near the end, it became a diplomatic effort again. After the war, the military played a secondary role and the diplomatic played a primary role under the Marshall Plan. That provided for a stable Europe for the next sixty years.

When you look at our four elements of national power and put them against the Global War on Terror, you begin to wonder: "What's the right amount to apply of each?" What's the equation needed to solve and win this global war?

You first have to really understand the cause of this war. Each war has different causes. This war is ultimately about the gap between the haves and the haves-not.

I talked earlier about not wanting to catch one fish at a time but to change the temperature of the water so that the fish we were after could no longer survive in that environment. And to do that you've really got to attack the causes of the frustration, not just the symptoms of the frustration. The symptoms of an unhappy society are people shooting at you, IEDs and riots. But the causes are much deeper, much more complicated and take a longer time to fix. You can end the symptoms by simply killing bad guys. But if you don't end the causes, the bad guys will simply regenerate, much like your own body when you're sick. You can lower your temperature by jumping in ice water but if you don't kill the bacteria, the temperature will simply rise again as soon as you get out. The high temperature is the symptom, the bacteria is the cause.

We tend to try the first three forms of power first — economic, information and diplomacy, as we should. But they have limits. The Department of Agriculture, Department of Labor, Department of State would have a hard time getting deployable employees who could go to Afghanistan and talk about how to have a viable wheat crop, talk about how to irrigate their land, talk about how to set up a business community and a chamber of commerce and real estate and legal systems and all the things that we take for granted in the West. A little bit of diplomacy, a little bit of information, a little bit of economics — all good — but hard to put on an airplane and send somewhere with a clear task and purpose.

Another problem: a spark gets caught in the wind and where it lands, nobody knows. But if the conditions are right, it'll create a massive fire. You can end up with fires all along a mountain range because of a couple of sparks. That's what the information and economic power have done across the Muslim world — inadvertently throwing sparks up in the air that, in many cases, land in potential hotbeds. You can turn military on and off, but it's hard to turn off information or economics. As an example, I ran into a boy in Afghanistan who was probably 13 or 14 years old and he was wearing a Dallas Cowboys T-shirt and a Marlboro Cigarettes baseball cap. That is really a confluence of information and economics. From his parents' perspective it is an informational assault onto their traditional Afghan culture. They couldn't stop it. America didn't deliberately launch Cowboy T-shirts and Marlboro cigarettes in Afghanistan. Who knows how they got there? But they got there. So our culture is being injected into basic roots all across the world, and it's not always welcome. That spark could be informational or economical.

I'm certainly ecstatic that bin Laden is now in his eternal resting place. But he was a symptom, not the cause. He was an opportunist who took advantage of the cause of that instability to promote himself to a position of power. Even with the symptom gone, the cause is still there.

The cause for the insurgency and the cause for the frustration and the cause for the millions of angry Muslim terrorists is still there.

These Afghan boys are eager to see the American visitors to their village. The kids would run alongside our vehicles barefoot, over the rocks. By the time they are about 10 or 12, if they survive that long, they are tough young men.

And that cause can only be eradicated by the proper use of the four elements of national power over a long-term approach. I asked my intelligence officer to answer one question for me: Why is everybody so bitter in this country, Afghanistan? And he came back with about seven or eight answers.

They're frustrated about the corrupt government, about the lack of medical care, about the lack of economic potential, about the lack of security, about the lack of education. Most of those are not military frustrations, but diplomatic, informational and economic issues. But those frustrations all build on each other so they boiled over, the pot boiled over. And the symptom of that frustration is attacks against the West.

The American mission in Afghanistan is really to do two things: for the short term, kill the bad guys now so they don't kill us first. Then for the long term, change the conditions so the society doesn't continually produce bad guys. The first one is fairly easy. That's simply an arithmetic problem. It's an application of force against moveable and non-moveable targets. It's a science problem. It's what our military does fairly well.

The second one, however, is the hard one. And that's what our conventional military doesn't do very well because our military is a blitzkrieg military designed for a different kind of war against a different kind of enemy with a different kind of thinking. Blitzkrieg means literally "lightning war." The military coined this phrase as the Germans unveiled their new tactic of quick, lightning invasions of Poland, France and all of Europe in 1939. I don't know whether many conventional leaders ask the question I did, and that is, "Why is everybody so angry?" Let's address that problem and then maybe some of these other problems will go away. I certainly recognize the need for killing bad guys. I fully support it and will do it myself if needed. It needs to be done. But that alone won't solve this particular problem. And that has to be solved with a different arithmetic equation from the traditional American way of war.

So that brings up the fourth element of national power, the military. The challenge with the elements of power is that the military is the only *expeditionary* element of those four powers—the only one of these four "powers" that can be deployed. You can organize a military, you can put them on a plane, you can deploy them for a particular task and purpose. That's what they do. Diplomatic, informational and economic elements, however, are much less expeditionary.

In fact, informational and economic elements of power almost work like a wildfire. Once a spark gets going economically or informationally, it's hard to stop regardless of what the national will is.

You can't turn it off and it's also hard to ramp it up. That's one of the greatest frustrations in the Arab world because Islam is basically a backward-looking religion, back to the seventh century A.D. when Mohammed walked the earth and it was a perfect time for that faith. Any deviation from that is against Allah's will. Mohammed didn't have T-shirts with Dallas Cowboys on them. Mohammed didn't have Marlboro baseball caps. Therefore, for the West, from the Muslims' perspective, to deliberately inject that kind of information into the youth in their society is almost an act of war. It is certainly an act of aggression that they don't want to tolerate.

We bring in the military to effect change when the other elements of national power don't work. The military is finite, has edges, can be controlled. No, we're not perfect, but we're not as subject to external whims as information or economics. The military is the expeditionary force and within the UW-capable Special Forces the military has some limited capability to use all elements of national power, including diplomatic, informational, and economic.

But it can't be done quickly. There's no blitzkrieg in an unconventional war. UW requires patience and time more than almost anything else. America is very blitzkrieg centric and very unconventional war phobic. But unfortunately in this war, the unconventional approach with the indigenous being the main effort is the definition of success. If we had realized that on a strategic level early, I think we would have been victorious years ago.

37

Provincial
Reconstruction Teams

When I was in Afghanistan we unveiled a new concept called PRT, Provincial Reconstruction Teams. The idea was that we'd put a small team of Americans in these provinces and help them create a more viable society. On the PRT would be all of these elements of power — diplomatic, informational, military, and economic. So we'd have an agricultural advisor, an education advisor, a business advisor, and a military security advisor — just a miniature snapshot of what a civilized society can do, which we thought was a great idea.

We laughed initially at the term "Provincial Reconstruction Team" when in fact it probably should have been a Provincial Construction Team since there wasn't a lot of reconstruction going on in a society that was fairly rudimentary to begin with. So we didn't necessarily reconstruct what they had. We actually wanted to construct. But we soon ran out of the non-military expertise to man the PRT. The military can constantly put soldiers in to provide security assistance and oversight and a limited number of civil affairs soldiers who understand the nexus between the military and civil society, but we currently have limits.

The elements of national power — diplomacy, information, and economics— are difficult to mobilize and deploy into a war zone. So the PRTs in many cases were predominantly manned by soldiers who simply had a non-military mission of helping the local economy or the local agriculture community or the local education community; all good and viable, all absolutely necessary. But the challenge is with the four elements of power. One is easily expeditionary and deployable, the other three are not. Yet, all four are equally important and must be on the shelf for potential use.

Americans want quick results. We all grew up in a drive-thru McDonald's society where you get it your way and you get it right away. Certainly the Middle Eastern and Asian cultures do not have such a short-term expectation. The American military in general is based on a mass blitzkrieg mentality. That mentality works well in the bulk of large conventional wars. But in this particular kind of war it's not applicable. We clearly blitzkrieged the Afghans from a military fire and maneuver perspective. That was not a challenge. But we're fighting for the will of the society to change the conditions of the environment, and blitzkreig just erases buildings.

I'm absolutely certain that the traditional military blitzkrieg mindset frustrated and limited our success in Afghanistan. We went in after 9/11 with a small unconventional force, the 5th Special Forces Group out of Ft. Campbell, Kentucky. Each of those Green Berets had been recruited, assessed, trained and qualified to work *by, with and through* the Afghan people.

They immediately worked with the locals, overthrew the Taliban, raised the Afghan flag in Kabul, and flew the U.S. flag over the U.S. Embassy there for the first time since President Carter was in office.

And then, three months later, a huge conventional force came in and began to conduct maneuverable warfare and kill bad guys. In the meantime, the causes of the locals' frustrations continued to grow.

The military does recognize that all things can't be solved by conventional firepower. Certainly there are a lot of smart people in the military. I'm not the first one to come up with this plan or the idea. The reality of it is that over the fifty years' existence of the Special Forces Regiment, there have been few instances where a conventional capability supports an unconventional objective.

What the army did was to create an unconventional capability so that it can ultimately support a large conventional war as opposed to the reverse. In Afghanistan, I actually had an unconventional capability that worked for a conventional campaign as opposed to the other way around, with conventional capabilities that can be used to support unconventional objectives if needed. That is what was, and is, needed to win this war.

America wants quick, decisive victories. You don't get quick, decisive victories working by, with and through others who look at the problems over decades or centuries. The unconventional approach requires patience. But patience is the critical vulnerability of our society. Centers of gravity are things that offer us strength, like our technology and economic advantage. Critical vulnerabilities are things that define our weaknesses. The critical vulnerability of this nation is our patience. The center of gravity for the enemy is their patience. It's a bad scenario. We try to attack their patience with quick, decisive wins that from their perspective are almost irrelevant. The enemy counterattacks with patience. Our politicians get restless. The enemy wins.

The fact that we blew into Kabul and occupied the U.S. Embassy and raised the flag in a couple of months was great. But the enemy simply downshifted into a lower gear, went deeper into the mountains and said, "Okay, we'll wait them out." And that's still what the enemy is doing today.

38

Learning from History

Now let's look at the opposite tack. *By, with and through.* Throughout history, one nation was extraordinarily good at using this to further their aims. The Brits were great at working through the locals, harnessing their natural talents and untold powers, changing from within for permanent change. Back in those days, the sun never set on the British Empire. But how did that come about? A tiny island nation with control over something like half of the world? The British were supreme commanders. The Brits were officers. But the middle managers were the Indians or the Pakistanis or the American colonials—the locals. And that's why all the countries that Britain colonized are in better shape today than the countries that anybody else colonized—the Portuguese, the Spanish, the Germans—because they harnessed the locals, they worked by, with and through. In other parts of the world under other conquerors, when the colonialists left they had nobody to take over. But the Brits kept the local populations as middle managers so that when the British colonialists left, it was a smaller step up from middle manager to manager.

I remember my meeting in Zimbabwe with the Minister of Defense. I was on a trip to Zimbabwe to do a "demining" assessment to see if we could help them take away some antipersonnel mines that had proliferated throughout the whole country. I had tea in the afternoon with the Minister of Defense of Zimbabwe, who was very dark-skinned, all African. We had high tea with scones at 3:00 in the afternoon.

He looked across his beautiful mahogany desk at me. He was wearing a starched uniform with three crowns on the shoulder for a general officer, same insignia as the British Empire, even though the Brits left Zimbabwe a long time ago, and he almost whispered to me and said, "I wouldn't say this in public, but we were very fortunate to have been colonized by Great Britain." I said, "Why is that?" He said, "Because they built up the locals as middle managers so that when they left, it was a smaller step for us to go up to the national leaders." That's a great lesson I learned as a young SF officer. That's what we ought to be doing, not as colonists but as leaders of the world. That's really the essence of democracy: to empower those who are not empowered by bringing them from servitude one step at a time up to reach and live up to their potential. He'd never been to Europe or America. His skin was black. Deep, dark Africa — yet, here we were drinking tea as if on the Queens's own china, and he was thankful to have been raised in a British colony. That is a successful UW strategy.

From our camps at Khost and A-bad I went to these border checkpoints on the Pakistan border and met the Pakistanis. I would meet with the Pakistani officers who look, other than their dark skin, more British than Brits — manicured, curly moustaches, blouses starched, riding crops, crowns on their insignias — just like the Brits. The Brits left there a long time ago. But they left an impact on Pakistan. The British Empire ended on the Afghan border. The last British square was in the Punjab area — the Khyber Pass. The "square" was a formation of His Majesty's soldiers with three or four ranks of riflemen facing in all four directions (thus the square). Given the technologies and tactics of the day, the square was undefeatable by cavalry or infantry. When that last British square was defeated in the Khyber Pass, the British Empire died as well.

On the one hand, I have an Afghan soldier who is hard as nails but looks like a cave man. He probably hasn't had ten baths in his life. Of course, no doctor, no dental care ... none of that. He's the colonel, so he might be able to read. And then I have a Pakistani soldier with a riding crop who smells like Old Spice and has his boys serving tea. And they live ten miles from each other. Night and day. British influence on one side, not on the other.

Even today the British Army has Gurkha regiments which are led by Brits and manned by Gurkhas. British regular Army officers will often do a tour commanding a Gurkha company. So that's the tradition, their whole army, their whole culture. Britain's the size of Kentucky, roughly. They don't produce that many men. How do they have so much international power? Strategic unconventional warfare, *by, with, and through,* for centuries! The British Empire ended after World War II. So why are they key players on the world stage? Because they wield power through surrogates. And that's unconventional warfare at the strategic level.

The sun still never sets on British influence.

The war in Afghanistan would have been picture-perfect for an unconventional strategy. Had we identified early on that we were going to focus on the indigenous people, we would have fought this war successfully. We'd have fewer American casualties and the enemy would have known early on that we would be in this for the long term. That creates allies, not enemies. That gets to root causes, not tubs of ice to fix symptoms. But we didn't do that because America doesn't do long-term commitments well, particularly in the face of events like 9/11. We like reciprocity of force, meet violence with violence. All good, but only a short-term solution.

It's never too late. But the time to determine the correct strategy is at the beginning of the war, not after ten years of the war. Our country has decided we're tired of fighting this war. So we're withdrawing our soldiers. As a smoke screen to that, we may try to increase the unconventional aspect and try to build up the indigenous capability. But really that's just so we can go home. It's entirely possible that at the end there's nobody left on the field but some Special Forces soldiers trying to reverse ten years of unilateral, conventional thinking.

What we have to do is shift our focus from ourselves to them. We have to shift from short-term goals to long-term patience. We have to use all elements of power, not just the military. Now that's hard, because, as I said, three of those elements have a hard time being expeditionary, three of those elements are hard to manage. But we need to send a clear message to the world that coming home is not our main priority; *victory in the global war against terrorism is our main priority!* Keeping Afghanistan out of the hands of the terrorists is our priority. Right now that would be hard to prove because we've proven the opposite for the last several years.

Again, back to the Tom Sawyer analogy—the road taken is that we paint the fence. The road not taken is to get everybody else to paint the fence. The indigs are willing, capable, able and motivated to paint the fence. They don't do it very well but that's okay. It doesn't have to be perfect. It just has to be done better than their enemies. That's the road not taken. And that was my default answer to every question, "Get them to do it." If we want permanent stability anywhere, we have to raise the indigenous capability to have that stability.

As I said in the beginning, you can't give people their freedom, they have to want it and earn it. Only then will they take over the concept and protect it with their lives. Only then will they turn away the terrorist training camps in favor of a safe world for their children. Freedom is a powerful tonic for what ails the world, but only when it is won by, with and through the people who surround you day in and day out.

39

Final Thoughts

I realized fairly early what my talents and abilities are and what they are *not*. So the question was, what was I going to do with these abilities? I wanted to make sure I invested them in something that was worthwhile, that would have a good return on investment for the Master.

I was fortunate to have found the military fairly early and realized that it was a pretty good match — my abilities and their prerequisites. I was very blessed to have found that match, and I hope I have reflected well upon God and the use of the talents that He has loaned me for this short duration.

Now, as normal people, we may not have a lot of talents; society can be the judge of that. But we all can determine how to invest our own talents. The world can judge how many talents we have but we're the ones who decide how they are used. I've tried to invest any abilities I had in worthy causes: protecting our Constitution from all enemies, both foreign and domestic, which is the oath I took thirty years ago— but also liberating the oppressed, which is the regimental motto of Special Forces, "de oppresso liber"—"to liberate the oppressed." And you liberate the oppressed by giving them the understanding and the ability to use their own talents to fill their own needs.

I was reared from childhood to go the extra mile — through all those football practices, all the Boy Scout hikes, all the big and small challenges, always to give it my all. When I realized our country needed people to do that professionally, I said just what I said to my many sports coaches, "Put me in, Coach. I'm ready." And that's what happened.

S.L.A. Marshall wrote a book called *Men Against Fire*. One of his conclusions was that men join the army for one reason but fight for another. He argued that we join the army for mom, apple pie and patriotism, but we fight and die for the guy next to us. Nobody dies for mom and apple pie. They die to help their buddy. That's as good as it gets. It doesn't get any better. "Greater love hath no man than this, that a man lay down his life for his friends," John 15:13 says. That's what pays for our freedom. That's how freedom perpetuates itself: the willingness of American soldiers to kill, fight and die. That's why we get tears in our eyes standing in front of the World War II memorial, the Korean War memorial, and at the Vietnam War memorial. We have tears for the men and women who died for all of us.

That's all we soldiers want out of our time in the service. Ultimately, that's why I made the Army my career: to protect our American freedom, to help our children and their children continue to enjoy that freedom, and to use my own talents to support that great cause. That's it. That's all. That was our mission. That was my mission.

Glossary

Ambush: A combat operation where the attacking force lies in wait for the defending force to move into the "kill zone."

AOR: Area of Operations. The geographic area assigned to a military unit for their operations.

A-team: Special Forces Detachment–Alpha. A twelve-man detachment commanded by a captain. The building block for America's Unconventional Warfare capability.

Auxiliary: The element of the insurgency tasked with providing at least passive support to the armed insurgent (guerrilla).

B-team: Special Forces Detachment–Bravo. The headquarters element of a Special Forces company commanded by a major and responsible for controlling six A-teams.

Civil Affairs: An element of Army Special Operations Command trained and organized to conduct operations to coordinate military and civil events and to develop civilian infrastructure in an occupied area. Most CA units are in the Army Reserve.

CJSOTF: Combined Joint Special Operations Task Force. *Combined* means multi-national, *Joint* means multi-service, *Special Operations* means the unit is made up of elements of USSOCOM, and *Task Force* is a temporary organization with a specific mission and duration. Most CJSOTFs are reinforced Special Forces Groups and commanded by an Army colonel.

COIN: The Army doctrine for counterinsurgency.

CT: Counterterrorist operations. CT is one of the several capabilities within Special Forces and the primary task for some units within USSOCOM.

Glossary

C-team: Special Forces Detachment–Charlie. The headquarters element of a Special Forces battalion commanded by a lieutenant colonel, responsible for controlling three B-teams and a Special Forces support company.

DA: Direct Action. The most common form of American combat, in which the U.S. service member takes direct action to unilaterally (without indigenous support) kill enemy soldiers. Most of USSOCOM has DA as their primary task. Special Forces is capable of DA operations, but has Unconventional Warfare as its primary task.

Guerrilla: The element of the insurgency that is the full-time armed combatant. He is supported by the auxiliary and the underground, much like the American infantryman is supported by support mechanisms ranging from the cooks in the headquarters to the training base back home. One of our goals was to separate the guerrilla from his support base by any means possible.

LP/OP: Listening post and observation post, a small group of soldiers placed on the perimeter of a military location tasked to listen and observe possible enemy movement near the location. LP OPs are typically well armed and equipped with communication in order to quickly pass pertinent information to the nearby post.

PSYOP: Psychosocial Operations soldiers are members of Army Special Operations Command tasked and organized to influence the actions of the enemy or civilian population using information and psychology as a weapon. They are not charged with stopping the enemy's *ability* to wage war; they are charged with stopping their *willingness* to wage war.

Raid: A combat operation in which the attacking force assaults the defending force. This is the sister operation of the ambush, where the defending force moves (unknowingly) into the assaulting force's area.

Rangers: The best light infantrymen on earth. Our Army has two types of Rangers: those who graduate from the two-month Ranger training course at Ft. Benning, Georgia; those assigned to the Ranger Regiment (75th Infantry), also headquartered at Ft. Benning. The Regiment consists of graduates of the Ranger course who have undergone significant additional individual and unit training for their specific task of quick, violent action against America's foes.

SEALs: Sea, Air and Land Sailors who are members of USSOCOM. SEALs are selected, trained, and organized for specific unilateral direct action operations against America's foes. Some SEALs are assigned to support the fleet; others are assigned to Special Operations organizations.

SF: Special Forces, known as the "Green Berets." The backbone of America's Unconventional Warfare capability. These Soldiers are recruited, assessed, trained, equipped and organized to fight America's wars "by, with and through" indigenous capabilities.

Underground: The element of the insurgency that supplies the logistical and popular support to the combat arm, the guerrilla.

USAFSOC: U.S. Air Force Special Operations Command, headquartered at Hurlburt Field, Florida. The command trains and organizes the Air Force element of the U.S. Special Operations Command.

USASOC: U.S. Army Special Operations Command is headquartered at Ft. Bragg, North Carolina. The command trains and organizes the Army element of the U.S. Special Operations Command. The command consists of Special Forces Command, the Ranger Regiment, the Special Operations Aviation Regiment, Civil Affairs and Psychological Operations Command, and the JFK Special Warfare Center and School.

USNAVSOC: U.S. Navy Special Operations Command, headquartered at San Diego, California. The command trains and organizes the Navy element of the U.S. Special Operations Command.

USSOCOM: America's combatant command for all Special Operations forces, commanded by a full (four-star) general with headquarters at McDill Air Force Base, Tampa, Florida. USSOCOM trains and organizes each of the services (Army, Navy, etc.) Special Operations Forces (SOF). In combat, SOF is normally commanded by the regional commander, not the US SOCOM commander.

UW: Unconventional Warfare. The art of war in which the main effort is focused on fighting the enemy "by, with and through" indigenous forces as opposed to fighting the enemy with primarily unilateral (American) forces.

Index

Index

Index

Index